MW01535325

CROCHET

•

THE BIBLE
5 books in 1

The Complete Guide to Master The Art of Crocheting With Step-By-Step Projects for Beginners, Intermediate and Advanced Including Amigurumi Patterns

By

Luna Stevens

TABLE OF CONTENTS

INTRODUCTION

With just a hook and some yarn, you can make lovely and useful things by crocheting, which is a terrific skill.

If you're like me who have spent over the past three years online, you've undoubtedly seen the rise in popularity of DIY apparel and accessories. Textile designs made from methods like crocheting, it enable everyone to create these made-at-home pieces and making your own wearable styles/design nearly—easy. Apart from the fact that crocheting is a stress reliever, it's also an excellent method to ignite your creativity. With this guide you'll be prepared to go out and make unique things for you and your entire family when you're done.

What Is Crochet?

A hook and yarn are used in the crocheting process to create textiles. Using your crochet hook, loop your working yarn continuously while crocheting. This produces a distinctive pattern that results in exquisite artwork known as crochet.

Despite popular belief, crocheting is much more than just making sweaters and washcloths. Thousands of practical and wearable pattern ideas have been created by independent and small businesses as a result of the popularity of social media sites like Pinterest and TikTok. Now, there's a good chance you can find a crochet design for everything you can think of.

Having experimented with both knitting and crocheting, I find that crocheting is a lot faster than knitting. Crocheting a beanie can be done in a few days, but knitting one may take many weeks. The primary reason for this is that crochet stitches are taller than knit stitches, however the size of the crochet hook and yarn used also plays a role. You get more out of each crochet Stitch since they have a larger surface area than knitted ones.

CROCHET SUPPLIES

The secret to learning to crochet is to select a lighter color yarn, choose a hook that complement it, and a smooth solid color yarn also.

Yarn

There are several weights, materials, and textures available in yarn. You'll start to like certain yarns over others on the long run, the more you use them and know more about them. When selecting yarn, be sure to thoroughly review your design and select a yarn that has the recommended weight.

Splits occur. While working with yarn, splits, also known as knots, are a regular occurrence. When this occurs, you have two options: cut your yarn and rejoin it using your favorite technique, or ignore the split and continue crocheting.

Hooks

There are many different types and sizes of crochet hooks. Look for the width measured in millimeters (mm) to determine the correct size. The size required to finish your project is listed under Crochet Patterns.

Scissors: You need this to cut your yarn.

The tapestry needle: this comes in handly at the end of your projects, it's used to weave the end part of your crochet project well, so it doesn't come off.

Stitch markers are a valuable tool for keeping track of stitches, particularly while crocheting in the round.

BOOK 1:

CROCHET IN GENERAL, STORY AND MAIN TECHNIQUES

Crocheting is a skill that requires relatively little knowledge to create beautiful things, yet there's always something new to learn. This is one of its greatest qualities. With just a little knowledge of materials and the fundamental single crochet stitch, you may create products such as blankets and scarves with ease. With the ability to learn more about materials, various stitches, multiple techniques, and pattern reading, you will be able to use your creativity to create absolutely unique objects. This guide will teach you the fundamentals of crochet, including a few common stitches, and will also give helpful hints to help you find more resources for further study.

The best part of crocheting that you don't hear often is the fact that you can get started with as little as a crochet hook and yarn.

SELECTING THE RIGHT YARN

Which sort of yarn should you get? It's quite OK to just try using the yarn you already have if you by hance have any at home. Having said that, some yarn are simpler to learn how to crochet with. The following are some items to check for if you are buying a yarn at the store:

a pale shade of a solid hue. You will find it more difficult to learn using yarn that is dark in color and that changes color throughout, since it will be more difficult to tell where your stitches should go.

See through to see how smooth the yarn is. These days, you may use any kind of fiber, and novelty yarns with various textures. All of them work well for crocheting, but when you're just starting out, you should use yarn with a more dull appearance. Although this yarn comes in varieties, fibers, wool, cotton, and acrylic are the most popular options. You can learn on with any of these, however get one that works for you. Cotton often has the highest Stitch definition, so it could be a good place to start. The definition of a Stitch is just the ability to see every shape in your crochet stitches. It is simpler to learn about things when they are plainly visible. Another excellent option that is also very reasonably priced is a really smooth acrylic.

A medium weight yarn. Both highly bulky and very thin yarn are available; in crocheting, each weight of yarn has a unique purpose and effect.

RIGHT CROCHET HOOK

It's okay to attempt learning with what you already have if you just so happen to have a crochet hook in your stockpile and don't want to spend money on new supplies. You can always use the hook you have and just get a yarn to start with. There are a few helpful things to know before buying your first crochet hook, though, whether you have to get a new one nonetheless or if you're finding it hard to learn with your current one.

Pick a hook size that matches the yarn you're using. In certain instances, the yarn label will include this information. You might also check this online. In theory, you may use any yarn and any size hook, but as a novice, using hooks intended for different yarn will be more challenging and yield drastically different results. Try using a size H crochet hook if you have chosen a medium weight yarn.

Note: The ideal hook to use with a particular yarn is usually listed on the packaging.

Choose a hook size that feel comfortable for you. Ideally, the suggested hook size for your yarn will feel appropriate, but if it doesn't, you can adjust a size up or down. Put another way, you could have decided to use a size G or size I crochet hook with your yarn, even if you may have started with a size H hook.

Important size information: Thread crocheting is done using incredibly small crochet hooks. If you plan to use standard yarn crochet hooks, gather additional information beforehand as the size on them is different.

Heads of Crochet Hooks. A crochet hook can have one of two typical "heads": an inline or tapered head. The inline shape is often deeper, flatter, and pointier than the tapered design. Learning more about the different styles and designs will happen latter on your journey. Right now, if you are struggling to learn to crochet, changing your crochet hook to a different one could make a difference.

Handles for crochet hooks. Hook handles come in a wide range of designs and materials (plastic and aluminum are the most popular, but there are also wood, bamboo, acrylic, and glass possibilities). Thumb grips are found on most crochet hooks, which makes crocheting simpler than with hooks without one. For those who have hand pain when crocheting, there are ergonomic handles available.

Best step to take right now is to select a medium-sized crochet hook made of plastic or aluminum, check to see whether it has a thumb rest, and take note of the hook head type in case you later decide you need to try a different sort.

HOW TO HOLD YOUR CROCHET HOOK

The most crucial thing to remember while holding your crochet hook is that you will need to experiment until you figure out the technique that works best for you. Apart from that, it's important to understand that there are two main ways that people hold their hooks: "like a pencil" and "like a knife." As their names imply, the way most people hold those two items is fairly similar to how you would hold the hook.

CROCHET HOOK PENCIL HOLD.

You hold the hook between your thumb and second finger while using the pencil grip. You may use your third finger to hold the hook, or you can curl it into your fist and offer further support.

CROCHET HOOK KNIFE HOLD.

Try starting with one of them, adjusting it to your comfort level, and if you still find it difficult, try the other technique using your own modifications. To observe exactly how you handle these objects, take some time to really pull a pencil out of a desk and a knife out of a drawer. Use this to practice holding your hook. Additionally, be aware that anything that seems strange at first will probably grow on you very soon.

CROCHETING IN ROUNDS VS. ROWS

The majority of crochet items are worked in rows or in the round. Crocheting in rounds, as the name implies, is starting with a circle and working your way out; hats, circular vests, and other round objects are frequently made using this technique. Crochet is done in rows, which means you work one row, then the next (usually turning the work, which will be covered in more detail later), to make square and rectangular objects like scarves and blankets. Shape-requiring items, like shawls, are often crochet in the round using increases and decrease. For now, the most essential thing to remember is that it is usually advisable to learn how to crochet rows before working on rounds.

The Slip Knot.

A slip knot is going to be used at the beginning of almost any crochet project. Certain distinctions exist, particularly when it comes to specialized crocheting abilities. The magic ring is a popular way to start tasks that are worked in the round rather than in rows. There are other methods that start with a slip knot, though, even when using that method.

Make sure the loose end of the yarn crosses over the top of the end that is still linked to your ball of yarn by bringing it into a loop.

Once the area where the yarn crossed over itself is in the center of the loop, pinch the top of the loop and bring it down vertically. At the end, you'll get something that looks like a pretzel.

Grab hold of the central yarn that passes through the "pretzel" vertically. Make it happen.

After pulling the yarn through, there will be a knot and a sizable loop above it.

Through the loop, insert your crochet hook going from right to left.

To make the loop tighter, tug on the yarn's loose end.

Now that you have your slip knot, start your crochet project in this process.

CROCHET A CHAIN

Most times you will start almost every crochet project you start with crocheting a chain. The first step to actually beginning to learn how to crochet is learning how to crochet a chain.

You might find that learning how to hold the yarn itself is odd at this point, even if you have become accustomed to using your crochet hook. It all comes down to the stress you feel when working with both hands. Recognize that you will adapt to it. Look for methods that suit your needs. Neither the yarn nor the crochet hook have proper or wrong ways to be held.

Yarn over.

It's better to understand this word now because you'll hear it a lot in crochet. "Yarn over" means to use the crochet hook's head to hold the working yarn—the part that is linked to the ball of yarn—in position while you bring it over the top of the hook. On occasions, it could be abbreviated as "YO."

It looks like this:

Slide the yarn that is still wound around the ball of yarn under the crochet hook's base.

Slide it over the crochet hook's top.

To grab it, bring it up beneath the hook's head.

Pull through.

Another crochet expression that you may hear a lot is "pull through." This implies that you bring the crochet hook from the back to the front of the work and pull the yarn that you have hooked onto it through the loop. That "yarn over" is being brought back through the same spot where the hook was first put. This is how that appears:

Draw the hook in the direction of the loop to the right.

Once the "yarn over" and hook head have fully passed through the loop, continue tugging the hook. That's your initial chain and where you should "yarn over" and "pull through."

To extend your chain, keep pulling the yarn over and again. this is your beginners chain.

SINGLE CROCHET

Since the single crochet Stitch is the simplest and most common fundamental Stitch to learn, we will start by going over how to work with it. However, when working rows of single crochet, it can occasionally be difficult to identify exactly where to put your hook due to its small length. Your best option is to skip down below and attempt learning one of the other fundamental crochet stitches first, preferably double crochet, if you are having trouble.

Let's start by dissecting the process of creating a single crochet stitch. It might be useful to know what a single crochet Stitch looks like since with crochet, you work one Stitch and then the one next to it. How to single crochet is as follows:

Put your hook through the chain.

It will become more important where you put the hook when you start working with various stitches and crocheting in rows. To start with, though, let's not worry about that for the time being. Just be aware that you will be pushing the hook through the Stitch from the front to the rear of the piece in order to insert it.

In the second Stitch from the hook, we will insert the hook. This is the method you will always begin a row of single crochet worked into your starting chain.

You will see that there will be two loops resting on top of the hook (and one strand of yarn beneath) as you enter the hook through the work, going from front to back. You've put the hook into the incorrect area of the Stitch if there aren't two loops on top of it. Reposition the hook and give it another try!

Yarn over, now.

pull through.

As with the beginning chain, you will succeed in "pulling through."

YO and draw two loops through the hook.

By now, you should have two loops from the single crochet stitch on your hook. This time, instead of attempting to "pull through," you're going to YO twice and pull it through the two loops on the hook.

This is how it appears:

Yarn over.

Pull through the hook's two loops.

You have now successfully finished your first single crochet after completing these instructions. Even if you already know how to make the single crochet stitch, there are a few useful things to brush up on.

Row of Single Crochet.

Creating a whole row of single crochet stitches, when you make your first single crochet stitch, you will work across the entire row of the chain you generated. Once you get to the last Stitch on the left side, you will repeat the previous steps in each Stitch of that starting chain one after the other.

In short, you will yarn over, place hook into next stitch, yarn over, pull through, YO and pull through both loops on hook, for your next single crochet. Then you'll do it again for the whole row.

Adding Single Crochet Rows.

As you reach the end of the row, you will need to form a turning chain. The beginning chain and the turning chain are constructed in the same manner. Depending on the sort of crochet Stitch you are using, the turning chain length will vary. It is one chain in single crochet. At the end of the row, you will have "chain one."

Turn the work to start your next row after creating your turning chain.

Turning the work is as easy as taking the left side, which has the turning chain, and flipping the entire piece horizontally so that the next row starts on the right side. When crocheting, you will most likely work from right to left, turn the piece, and then work from left to right once again.

Next, you will work a single crochet into each Stitch all the way across the row. To help you visualize where to put your crochet hook after you complete each stitch. You should insert the hook such that the two loops lie on top of the loop, as there are two loops.

example:

Go the other way in the row.

To add more rows, add your turning chain, turn your work, and repeat single crochet stitches across the row.

As you work on the first row, be sure to keep track of how many single crochet stitches you create. Stitch markers are little devices that you insert every ten or so stitches to aid in maintaining stitch count throughout a long row.

You need to know the number of single crochet stitches in the first row in order to keep the item you are making square or rectangular. For each row that follows, you want the same quantity. As a result, if you have ten single crochet stitches in row 1, you should have 10 in row 2.

This is when that "turning chain" comes into play. That chain is the first single crochet of the row. You will begin your second single crochet in the stitch next to it, not in the first stitch of the row underneath it. You should conclude that row with the same number of stitches as you started, counting the turning chain as one of those threads.

If there are 10 stitches in the first row, you should start by crocheting your turning chain, which counts as the initial single crochet stitch. Thereafter, you will work nine more single crochet stitches to finish the row, making 10 in all.

A COMMON MISTAKE

It is quite possible for your count to be incorrect, in which case you would receive an uneven shape rather than a square. People usually add stitches or don't have enough stitches in a row because they are unsure of exactly where to place their hooks. It is crucial to keep tabs on each row for this reason. The most frequent error is starting a row with an extra stitch; because the turning chain counts as the first stitch, you should always start in the second stitch. The other typical error is failing to add the last stitch; occasionally, it might be difficult to notice and you overlook it. Maintain count, use Stitch markers if necessary, and go back and redo anything you think is incorrect as soon as you notice it.

When you crochet, you can simply rip back your work by taking out your hook, pulling on the yarn, and letting it unravel until you're ready to pick up where you left off. This is sometimes referred to as "frogging" in crochet, a word that is derived from the similarity between the sounds "rip it, rip it" and "ribbit, ribbit."

TERMS AND MEANING

alt: alternate

approx: approximately

beg: begin/beginning

bet: between

bl/blo: back loop/back loop only

bo: bobble

BP: back post

BPdc: back post double crochet

BPtdr: back post double treble crochet

BPhdc: back post half double crochet

BPsc: back post single crochet

BPtr: back post treble crochet

CA: color A

CB: color B

CC: contrasting color

ch: chain stitch

ch-: refer to chain or space previously made, e.g., ch-1 space

ch-sp: chain space

CL: cluster

cont: continue

dc: double crochet

dc2tog: double crochet 2 stitches together

dec: decrease

dtr:double treble crochet

edc: extended double crochet

ehdc: extended half double crochet

esc: extended single crochet

etr: extended treble crochet

FL/FLO: front loop/front loop only

foll: following

FP: front post

FPdc: front post double crochet

FPdtr: front post double treble crochet

FPhdc: front post half double crochet

FPsc: front post single crochet

FPtc: front post treble crochet

hdc: half double crochet

hdc2tog: half double crochet 2 stitches together

hk: hook

inc: increase

lp: loop

m: marker

MC: main color

md(s): round(s)

mm(s): millimeter(s)

pc: popcorn stitch

pm: place marker

prev: previous

ps/puff: puff stitch

rem: remaining

rep: repeat

rnd: round

RS: right side

sc: single crochet

sc2tog: single crochet 2 stitches together

sh: shell

sk: skip

sl st: slip stitch

sm/sl m: slip marker

sp: space

st: stitch

trtr: triple treble crochet

tbl: through back loop

tch: turning chain

ws: wrong side

tog: together

yo: yarn over

tr: treble crochet

yoh: yarn over hook

tr2tog: treble crochet 2 stitches together

OTHER BASIC CROCHET STITCHES

The single crochet stitch serves as the foundation for a number of other fundamental crochet stitches. Recall the sc "yarn over"? Basically, you may achieve comparable crochet stitches of varying heights by adding additional "yarn overs.".

HALF DOUBLE CROCHET

The half double crochet, or hdc, St is crochet in a manner very similar to that of the sc St with the exception of starting with an additional "yarn over," which gives the St a little bit more height than the single crochet. The hdc is worked as follows:

Start with a foundation chain that has the appropriate length.

Yarn over: From back to front, wrap the yarn around the hook.

The third chain from the hook is where you should place your crochet hook.

(YO) AGAIN.

Three loops are created on the hook as the yarn is pulled through the chain stitch.

(YO)AGAIN.

With only one loop remaining on the hook, draw the yarn through all three of the loops.

One hdc St has been accomplished.

For every St along the row, repeat steps 3 through 8.

Turn your work and chain two when you reach the end of the row.

Working Hdc Rows

Throughout the row, you will keep working in hdc stitches. When you get to the end, you will chain two for the turning chain. Remember that the length of your turning chain is determined by the height of your crochet stitches. You would chain one for a single crochet and two for a half double crochet.

Turn the work and repeat the hdc stitches across the next row, making sure that you have the same amount of stitches in each row as you did in the previous rows.

DOUBLE CROCHET

One of the most used crochet stitches is the dc stitch. It's the main St in the traditional square pattern, which is a popular crochet motif, and may be used to create a wide variety of patterns. The acronym "dc" stands for double crochet.

Dc is comparable to half double crochet, with the exception that it starts with a yarn over. It differs from the half dc St in that it has an additional yarn down the line, making it even higher. Let's examine the creation of the dc stitch:

Start with a foundation chain that has the appropriate length.

Yarn over: From back to front, wrap the yarn around the hook.

Your crochet hook should be inserted into the fourth chain from the hook.

(YO)AGAIN.

Three loops are created on the hook as the yarn is pulled through the chain stitch.

(YO)AGAIN.

Leaving two loops on the hook, draw the yarn through the first two loops.

(YO)once again.

With only one loop remains on the hook, draw the yarn through the other two loops.

One dc St has been accomplished.

For every St along the row, repeat steps 3 through 10.

Turn your work and chain three (for your turning chain) when you reach the end of the row.

Working it

Throughout the row, you will work dc stitches. Chain 3 to create your turning chain when you reach the end of the row. Flip your project. Work dc stitches in each St throughout the row, starting in the second stitch.

TREBLE CROCHET

Compared to the double crochet, the treble crochet is taller. Instead of treble crochet, it is frequently referred to as the "triple crochet" denoted as "tr."

With the exception of starting with an extra (YO) to give it height, the treble crochet St is done nearly precisely like the dc stitch. By now you should be beginning to feel comfortable enough to handle this enjoyable St in crochet. This is how to crochet it:

Start with a foundation chain that has the appropriate length.

Twice, from back to front, wrap the yarn over the hook.

From the hook, omit the first three chains.

Your crochet hook should be inserted into the fourth chain from the hook.

(YO) AGAIN.

After putting the yarn through the chain stitch, the hook will have four loops.

(YO) AGAIN.

Leave three loops on the hook after passing the yarn through the first two loops.

(YO) AGAIN.

Leaving two loops on the hook, draw the yarn through the next two loops.

(YO) AGAIN.

With only one loop remaining on the hook, draw the yarn through the final two loops.

One treble crochet St has been accomplished.

For every St along the row, repeat steps 4 through 12.

When you reach the end of the row, chain four and turn your work.

Working the Rows

You will perform treble crochet stitches in every St along the row, as you have realized. Finish the row by rotating the work and chaining 4 for the turning chain to begin the following row. Your chain 4 is the first treble crochet of the following row.

You may continue to grow larger and taller than treble crochet by using the same general process.

Instead of starting with two yarnovers, a "double treble" starts with three, a "triple treble" with four, etc. Nevertheless, these longer stitches are more difficult to learn and are not frequently used due to the strain of having to hold that much yarn on the hook.

DOUBLE TREBLE

Start with a foundation chain that has the appropriate length.

(YO) the hook three times, working backwards to forwards.

From the hook, omit the first four chains.

The fifth chain from the hook is where you should place your crochet hook.

(YO) AGAIN.

Create five loops on the hook by weaving the yarn through the chain stitch.

(YO) AGAIN.

Leaving four loops on the hook, draw the yarn through the first two loops.

(YO) AGAIN.

Leaving three loops on the hook, draw the yarn through the next two loops.

(YO) AGAIN.

Leaving two loops on the hook, draw the yarn through the next two loops.

(YO) AGAIN.

With only one loop remaining on the hook, draw the yarn through the final two loops.

One double treble crochet St has been accomplished.

For every St along the row, repeat steps 4 through 14.

Turn your work and chain five (for your turning chain) when you reach the end of the row.

MAGIC RING

Start by encircling your hand with your yarn so that the longer end, which goes toward the yarn ball, crosses over the shorter end.

After then, take your fingers out of the loop while maintaining a firm grip on the crossed-over portion.

To create a new loop, pull the yarn that was crossed across through the loose loop.

With the loop beneath, firmly grasp the freshly created loop. Hook your hook through the freshly created loop (swap the hands holding the loop first).

Now, much like you would normally crochet, wrap your yarn around your non-hook hand. To generate tension, now insert your pinky and ring fingers into the loop. Some crocheters become disappointed because they forget to complete this step. Make sure your fingers are included in the loop.

Now chain the required amount of starting chains so that you may start your first stitch.

Work your stitches into the magic circle (around the loop you formed of yarn) at this point. When crocheting, make sure your ring and pinky fingers stay in the circle.

You must take your fingers out of the ring and pull the short end of the yarn (yarn end) once you have completed crocheting all of your stitches into the magic circle required for the first round.

Pull the end of the yarn until the circle closes all the way. Normally, I weave in this end as soon as I begin the second round of crocheting, but first I make sure it is knotted somewhere to prevent it from coming free later.

You have just produced a magical ring. Very simple, right?

HOW TO CROCHET POST STITCHES

There are many interesting things to learn after you grasp the basic crochet stitches. One of the things that may add the most texture and detail to your work is learning how to crochet post stitches. Post stitches, as opposed to regular stitches, are stitched around the St rather than into its loops. This technique creates practically three-dimensional effects in flat crochet, such as basketweave and crochet cables.

How to Front Post Double Crochet

The name of a stitch while working with post stitches is determined by the type of stitch and whether it is worked around the front or back of the post. First, let's take a look at front post double crochet, or just fpdc for short, which is a dc St crocheted around the front of a post.

We are now working with a standard dc St and will soon start working with a front post double crochet. You will (YO) just like you would with a standard double crochet.

Simply go on with your dc as usual at this point. Yarn over, please.

Make it through. Keep in mind that, because you've worked around the post, you might need to raise the loop slightly to get the standard dc St height; with experience, this will seem more natural.

(YO) AGAIN.

Make it through. By now, it ought to be beginning to resemble the dc St that you are accustomed to.

YO and draw both loops on the hook through. You have now successfully completed your front post double crochet. Although the St is crocheted around the post, it should appear like a standard dc stitch.

HOW TO BACK POST DOUBLE CROCHET

You may, of course, St a dc around the back post rather than the front post.

In the same manner, you will start by turning the yarn over to form a dc stitch.

Once more, enter the hook from right to left, but this time, above the post, so the crochet hook sits on top of the post. This St is called a "back post" St because the post is "back" of the hook.

Continue your dc St as usual to finish it. The St next to the one on the right is a bpdc done around the post, and you can see in the upper photo that it is a conventional dc worked in the loops. Here, you can see the exact location of the back post St in relation to the cloth.

FRONT LOOP ONLY WITH BACK LOOP ONLY

The first step in learning to crochet is to put your crochet hook through both loops of a stitch. As you become more skilled, though, you'll see that you can also work into just one loop of any fundamental crochet St to produce a variety of effects. Depending on which St you are working into, this crochet is referred to as "front loop only" (FLO) or "back loop only" (BLO).

Front Loop Only Crochet

Working into the front loop only (abbreviated FLO) of a crochet is possible.

Only the arm of the "v" nearest to you, or the "front" of the work, should be entered through with your hook when working FLO crochet. As always, you will enter the hook through this single loop and then proceed to work your way back toward the front of the piece. The other arm of the "v" will be behind the loop that you have one on your hook.

Now let's examine FLO single crocheting. You need to (YO) now that you've already put your hook into the front loop only.

you're still performing a conventional single crochet; the only thing that's different is where you placed the hook at first.

To finish the FLO single crochet, you will now need to (YO) and pull through the loops on the hook.

There you have it—a row of front loop only sc works.

Back Loop Only Crochet

The hook is inserted into the back loop of the St rather than the front loop when crocheting in the back loop only.

Hook your hook into the arm of the "V" at the "back" of the work, or the arm that is furthest from you. If not, carry out your St as usual.

FLO vs BLO Crochet

Although it may be difficult to distinguish between front loop only & back loop only crochet stitches when working numerous rows at once, they have distinct consequences. Compared to when you work in both loops, both alternatives will alter a piece's texture, but they each do it in a different way.

Although the texture shift is a little less noticeable with front loop only crochet than with back loop only crochet, you still get some wonderful lines throughout the work that provide a playful design element. FLO is an excellent option when you want an item to have stretch to it since it produces a stretcher fabric than working in either the back loop only or both loops.

More texture may be seen with back loop only crochet; it nearly seems as though one row is standing straight up behind another. BLO is frequently used to provide a ribbed effect.

HOW TO INCREASE IN CROCHET ROWS

In crochet, increasing is rather easy. All it indicates is that you are working on a row that has more stitches than the row below it by adding stitches to the row. Working many stitches into a St from the row below accomplishes this.

Naturally, a crochet increase is not limited to double crochet; it may be worked in any of the fundamental stitches. Almost usually, they are stitched in the same St as the row as a whole. you would work two single crochets into the same St if you had a row of single crochets with an increase.

Alternatively, you may make two hdc stitches into one St if you wanted to increase in hdc. Depending on where you want your shaping to occur, increasing can occur anywhere in the row, though it usually does so at the start or finish of the row. The crochet pattern you are working with will indicate where to make the increases. Even though it may not always be stated, you can tell it is an increase since you are working two stitches into one St if you see anything like "2 dc in next stitch."

HOW TO DECREASE IN CROCHET ROWS.

Reducing in rows is a little more challenging. The fundamental stitches will remain the same, but you will need to modify them somewhat.

When you decrease, you are taking fewer stitches in a row, making the row you are working on have less stitches than the row below. Working one St across two stitches from the preceding row accomplishes this. You start a St and don't finish it, then you start a new St in the St next to it and don't finish it, and finally you finish the two stitches together. This provides you the decrease but, in effect, changes two stitches at the bottom into one St at the top, giving you the same height as all the other stitches in the row. We'll examine how to reduce in three distinct foundational stitches: half double crochet, double crochet, and single crochet.

How to Decrease Sc

Let us first examine the process of decreasing in a sc stitch.

Yarn over. You would start a standard sc St in this manner.

Now you would (YO) again, pull through, and be done, just like you would with a standard sc stitch. But for the time being, you will begin the second sc St and leave the previous one incomplete. Now that you have two loops on your hook, go ahead and hook onto the next stitch.

Yarn over, again.

Make it through. Three loops will now be attached to your hook. There are the starting stitches for two distinct single crochets side by side, but none is finished. To finish them, add the top section to each at the same time, decreasing the St count by decreasing two sc stitches into one St at the top.

Yarn over, again.

Once you have pulled through every loop on the hook, you have joined the two threads into a single stitch. You are now down to one crochet.

HOW TO DECREASE HDC

Let's now examine this with the higher stitch, hdc.

Starting with a yarn over, you will work in half double crochets just like any other.

Hook into the following stitch.

YO, now.

Make it through.

YO, again. For the time being, we're going to leave the first half dc incomplete and start the second hdc. If this were a typical hdc stitch, you would be pulling through the loops on the hook to finish the stitch.

Hook into the following stitch.

YO, again.

Make it through. You now have two hdc stitches started side by side, but they are not quite complete. Now let's combine them to make a connected half double crochet, which is a decrease.

YO, please.

Make sure to pull through every loop on the hook. Three hdc stitches, a half dc decrease, and two additional regular hdc stitches are shown in the above picture, going from right to left.

HOW TO DECREASE DOUBLE CROCHET

This is the dc method for decreasing.

(YO) is the initial step, and this is how you would begin your next double crochet.

You continue double crocheting as usual, working the hook into the next stitch.

(As usual), you'll yarn over.

And pull through (this is still a standard dc).

And repeat the yarning.

Up until now, everything of stuff has been dc as usual. That is, however, where things diverge. To finish the stitch, you would now YO and pull through one more, just like you would with a regular double crochet. To reduce, however, you must leave the St incomplete for the time being. You'll see that the hook has two loops.

You're going to start spinning yarn again.

To start the second of the two dc stitches, you will insert the hook into the St after drawing through the final two loops on the hook.

YO again so you will keep working this second stitch.

When you pull through, the hook will display four loops.

YO, please.

Pull through the hook's initial two loops. There will now be three loops remaining on the hook. The key point to note is that you now have two finished dc stitches side by side, each requiring one more loop to be completed on top. The way you decrease the two stitches into one St is to make that one loop together on both of them.

Yarn over, please.

Make sure to pull through every loop on the hook. The images above show that there are two dc stitches, a reduced double crochet, and then additional standard dc stitches, working from right to left.

READING CROCHET PATTERNS

Crochet patterns are an excellent way to pick up new stitches and make lovely things. My patterns are all written in simple English, as if I were seated next to you. However, some patterns could appear overpowering. You'll quickly become proficient at reading and adhering to patterns with a little practice.

Standard abbreviations are used in most crochet patterns to indicate the various stitches. The following are a few of the most often used acronyms in crochet patterns:

ch: chain

sc: single crochet

dc: double crochet

hdc: half-double crochet

tr: treble crochet

While some printed patterns and instructions do not call for gauge of any kind, many do. In that instance, it is important to pay attention to the gauge, or the quantity of stitches and rows per inch, when reading a crochet design. To make sure that the thing you produce will be the right size, gauge may be quite important.

BOOK 2:
STEP-BY-STEP PROJECTS FOR BEGINNERS

You can actually produce a lot of things after you are somewhat comfortable working with your materials and have mastered the slip knot, ch, and anyone of the fundamental crochet stitch. You may practice learning these stitches by creating anything that comes to mind that is square or rectangle.

To get started, simply select a project. Assume you wish to create a scarf or a washcloth.

Crochet a ch that is roughly the desired project's width—possibly a little bit longer—and lengthen it.

Choose your St. Insert your initial St into the appropriate chain segment. Work your first dc, for instance, into the third ch from the hook if you're using dc. Next, continue working dc stitches into each chain until the finish.

Turning chain in crochet. Ensure that the turning chain's length matches the St you have selected; for example, if you are working in dc, the turning chain will be chain 3. Rotate the task. Throughout the row, dc into every stitch.

To make the object as long as you want it to be, repeat the previous step until it is square for a washcloth or extremely long for a scarf.

CROCHET A SCARF

Scarfs are a great first crochet project since they are so simple and enjoyable. They are easy to create and a wonderful present for loved ones.

Crocheting a scarf is probably the next step once you've mastered the basic techniques. You may make excellent use of your freshly gained crocheting abilities. Just learning crochet stitches without seeing the finished product may get rather monotonous.

But what if, even as a complete novice, you could create something exquisite and incredibly practical? Giving someone handmade presents for their birthday or Christmas truly makes a difference.

In essence, a crochet scarf is a long rectangle that requires no increases or decrease.

This makes it a very easy craft to do, even for a complete crochet novice. It's quick and enjoyable.

Before you even take up your crochet hook, there are a few things you should think about. There are several methods for creating a simple scarf. It will be simpler to complete your scarf if you have a detailed strategy in advance.

First, you must choose whether to crochet your scarf widthwise or lengthwise.

You will just need to crochet a few rows if you choose to crochet your scarf lengthwise. But they will be long rows with plenty of stitches.

Because you'll be working on shorter rows, crocheting a scarf widthwise is a little simpler. To get the required length, you will need to use a couple of them, though.

Selecting the appropriate St is the next step. You can select a lacy, flat, or textured stitch. It is imperative that you select a St that both suits your intended completed result and you as a worker.

Finally, think about the final product you wish to create. You can continue with the excellent endeavor of creating a traditional scarf. Alternatively, you may St the two ends together to create an infinite scarf.

What you need

Not many supplies are needed to crochet a scarf. You will want a yarn that is appropriate for novices. Ideally, the yarn should be very thick or bulky, easy to see through, and work with. Additionally, it progresses swiftly, providing immediate gratification upon project completion.

Second, a decent crochet hook of the appropriate size is required. You should start by using the hook size that is suggested on the yarn label. You will eventually learn how to match the size of the hook to your tension.

To weave the ends in, you will also need a tapestry needle large enough for the bulky or extra bulky yarn.

A nice pair of sharp scissors can help you cut your yarn neatly and thread the needle more easily.

A decent tape measure is essential since we will need to measure the crochet scarf's width and length.

Choose a St that you enjoy working with and utilizing. This St ought to be compatible with the yarn as well.

The finished size of your crochet scarf must be decided upon before you begin. Six inches is the most common scarf width. This is entirely a matter of preference, though, since some individuals like them narrower or broader.

An adult crochet scarf should ideally measure 60 inches in order to fit them comfortably.

MAKE SIMPLE SCARF WIDTHWAYS

a basic scarf widthways crocheted in short rows.

Making a slip knot is the first step in creating the foundation chain.

Next, chain the number of stitches required to reach 6 inches. Next, add an additional chain since we're going to begin crocheting into the second ch from the hook.

Work backwards in the first row along the foundation chain. Working into the rear bump of the foundation chain is my preferred method since it neatens the edge and matches the top edge. Work 1 sc into the beginning chain and continue working into each chain stitch.

To get the desired finishing size, follow the measurements rather than worrying about gauge or tension at this time. Fit is a fairly forgiving aspect of crocheted scarves.

All you need to do now is work in rows of sc stitches until the required length is reached.

On the edges of the rows, St markers are another option. Knowing where your first and last st are will be made easier by this. in order to avoid misplacing them and having a crooked scarf.

When your crochet scarf reaches the desired length, fasten it off and snip the yarn, leaving a longer tail. To be able to weave in the end, I normally allow around ten inches. In order to prevent your scarf from falling apart, you must tightly weave in the ends.

To safely complete the last stitch, thread the yarn tail through the tapestry needle and pass it through the final loop in a manner similar to a sl st.

Thread the yarn through the St tunnel using your tapestry needle. To increase the friction, you also need to divide the yarn and thread it through each leg of the stitches. This implies that you shouldn't undo your ends.

You must return in the opposite way and do a few back-and-forth zigzag rows, or around three to four rows.

To avoid giving the scarf an uneven form, avoid pulling the yarn too tightly.

You may now, if you'd like, add some fringe to the scarf's ends to give it an even more unique look.

INFINITY SCARF

To get started you need:

A yarn.

5.0 mm hook

scissors

tapestry needle

Average Size fits most: 68 (circumference) x 3.5 (width) inches

Instruction

Create a ch of 186 and use a slip St to join the first and last ch.

In order to crochet the back bump, begin at the second ch from the hook and work one St each ch: *1 sc, 1 dc, repeat from.

Don't slip St until the very end because you will now be crocheting in continuous rounds.

R2-11: *1 sc, 1 dc, continue from * until round 11 is finished, then sl st.

Every St starts with a single crochet, and the next St is always a double crochet. In addition, to get the incredible texture and appearance of a lemon peel, you crochet a dc on top of a sc and vice versa.

When you're done, weave in the ends and fasten off.

CROCHET COWL

To create a circle, the scarf is crocheted flat, sewn together longitudinally. There is a double twist connecting the cowl.

Instead of using a foundation chain, this pattern makes use of foundation half dc stitches. This makes the edge more flexible.

You can also build a foundation chain, but for the chain, I suggest using a larger size (7mm) crochet hook. This is a result of foundation chains' propensity to be marginally tighter and less flexible than other chains. More flexibility is produced and more space between the links is created when you use a little larger size hook for the chain.

There is no St count for the Ch 1 at the start of a row.

By adjusting the chain length, you can build a shorter or longer scarf.

By working more or fewer rows, you can create a scarf that is wider or narrower.

If you are beginning with foundation hdc stitches, work 86 foundation HDC stitches, or until you reach 28 inches, using the 6mm hook.

Proceed to Row 2.

If you are beginning with a foundation chain, start with a 7mm crochet hook and work your way up to 88 chains, or until your chain is 28 inches long. Then, switch to a 6mm hook. Work an HDC while working on the back side of your chain by putting your hook in the third Ch (bump) from the hook. Work HDC in each Ch to the end of the row.

Row 2 – 33 (12.5 inches, or until you reach your desired width): Turn to Ch 1. Work HDC in each St throughout the row, including the third loop of the initial stitch. Don't forget to complete the last stitch! Every row should include the same number of st.

When the scarf has reached the required width, tie off and snip the yarn, leaving about a 35-inch tail to St the sides together.

Putting the Cowl together.

Once the appropriate width is achieved (33 rows for this cowl), place it flat on a table and insert the yarn needle. Take the cowl and twist it twice on one side. Ensure that the rows on both sides match when you St the two sides together.

Once all ends are woven in, finish!

BOHO BOBBLE TWIST HEADBAND

With your H 5.0mm crochet hook, make a slip knot.

Row 1: Foundation hdc 57 CH 1. Turn your work.

Row 2: SC 7, *Bobble, SC* across for 43 total stitches. SC 7. CH 1. Turn your work. Size 57

Row 3: HDC across. CH 1. Turn your work. (size 57)

Row 4: HDC in the camel hump across. CH 1. Turn your work. (size 57)

Rotate your work forward (away from you) and find the loop right under the "v" where you usually place your hook to identify the camel hump. YO, put your hook from the bottom to the top of the loop. This will create a knit-like texture by pushing your "v" loops towards the right-side of your headband, where the bobble stitches emerge. Put your HDC in that spot.

Row 5: HDC in the camel hump across. CH 1. Turn your work. (size 57)

Turn your work in your direction and look for the loop that is directly beneath the "v," where you usually place your hook, to identify the camel hump. Hey, put your hook in that loop from top to bottom. This will create a knit-like texture by pushing your "v" loops towards the right-side of your headband, where the bobble stitches emerge.

Row 6: SC 7, *Bobble, SC* across for 43 total stitches. SC 7. CH 1. Turn your work. (size 57)

Row 7: HDC across. CH 1. Turn your work. (size 57)

Row 8: HDC in the camel hump across. CH 1. Turn your work. (size 57)

Row 9: HDC in the camel hump across. CH 1. Turn your work. (size 57)

Row 10: SC 7, *Bobble, SC* across for 43 total stitches. SC 7. CH 1. Turn your work. (size 57)

Row 11: HDC across. CH 1. Turn your work. (size 57)

Row 12: HDC in the camel hump across. CH 1. Turn your work. (size 57)

Row 13: HDC in the camel hump across. CH 1. Turn your work. (size 57)

Row 14: SC 7, *Bobble, SC* across for 43 total stitches. SC 7. CH 1. Turn your work. (size 57)

Row 15: HDC across. CH 1. Do not cut your work. (57)

Making the Twist

Just to ensure that your work doesn't unravel when you set your hook down, pull up a lengthy loop.

When the bobble stitches are in contact with one another, fold the two ends of your creation in half like a hot dog.

Next, put them inside each other.

You're using the four ends of your headband to create a zigzag-like pattern.

To retain your work in the sandwiched position, use some sort of clip.

Right now, the upper right corner should have your working yarn. Re-enter the loop that you left on your working yarn with your hook.

We will now slip St our sandwiched ends together, enclosing the raw edges. Since this is the unfinished edge of our work, you will need to create your own slots for your hook.

To complete one SL ST, insert your hook through each of the four walls of our zigzag sandwich, then pull through all of the stitches and the loop on your hook.

Pull through all of the stitches and loops on your hook by inserting your hook into the next spot and passing through all four walls once more, YO. It's the second SL ST you have.

Continue sewing the ends of your zigzag sandwich together by slip stitching them together.

Tighten the knot to seal the end. Put your tails in. Turn your headband around so that it becomes a bohemian bobble twist headband!

STORMBORN WRAP

Materials

- Yarn
- 6mm Hook
- Bent Tip Tapestry Needle
- Scissors

Measurements: 173 x 74 cm/ 68 x 29"

GAUGE: 10cm/4" square = 13.5 stitches wide x 8 rows tall in double crochet

Terms:

Ch = Chain

Sl st = Slip Stitch

SC = Single Crochet

DC = Double Crochet

Bobble = Bobble Stitch

Ch-sp = Chain Space

St(s) = Stitch(es)

Rep = Repeat

Sk = Skip

Instructions:

To start, work a magic loop or double magic loop by working ch 4 and sl st into the first ch to make a ring.

Row 1: Start by chaining 3, then make 2 double crochets. Chain 2 to create the center space and then make 3 more double crochets. Turn your work.

Row 2: Chain 3, make 2 double crochets into the first stitch, double crochet 2 more times. In the center space, work a double crochet, chain 2, and another double crochet. Then double crochet 2 more times and finish with 3 double crochets in the last stitch. Turn your work.

Row 3: Chain 3, make 2 double crochets into the first stitch, followed by double crocheting 5 more times. In the center space, work a double crochet, chain 2, and another double crochet. Continue with double crochets 5 more times, and end with 3 double crochets in the last stitch. Turn your work.

Row 4: Chain 3, make 2 double crochets into the first stitch, double crochet 8 more times. In the center space, work a double crochet, chain 2, and another double crochet. Continue with double crochets 8 more times, and finish with 3 double crochets in the last stitch. Turn your work.

Row 5: Chain 3, make 2 double crochets into the first stitch, followed by double crocheting 11 more times. In the center space, work a double crochet, chain 2, and another double crochet. Continue with double crochets 11 more times, and end with 3 double crochets in the last stitch. Turn your work.

Row 6: Chain 3, make 2 double crochets into the first stitch, double crochet 14 more times. In the center space, work a double crochet, chain 2, and another double crochet. Continue with double crochets 14 more times, and finish with 3 double crochets in the last stitch. Turn your work.

Row 7: Chain 3, make 2 double crochets into the first stitch, double crochet once, then chain 1, skip 1 stitch, and double crochet. Repeat this pattern until you reach the center space. In the center space, work a double crochet, chain 2, and another double crochet. Then, continue with chain 1, skip 1 stitch, and double crochet until you reach the last stitch, where you'll make 3 double crochets. Turn your work.

Row 8: Chain 3, make 2 double crochets into the first stitch. Double crochet in each stitch and chain space until you reach the center space. In the center space, work a double crochet, chain 2, and another double crochet. Then, double crochet in each stitch and chain space until you reach the last stitch, where you'll make 3 double crochets. Turn your work.

Row 9: Chain 3, make 2 double crochets into the first stitch. Double crochet 23 more times. In the center space, work a double crochet, chain 2, and another double crochet. Continue with double crochets 23 more times, and end with 3 double crochets in the last stitch. Turn your work.

Row 10: Chain 3, make 2 double crochets into the first stitch. Double crochet 26 more times. In the center space, work a double crochet, chain 2, and another double crochet. Continue with double crochets 26 more times, and finish with 3 double crochets in the last stitch. Turn your work.

Row 11: Chain 3, make 2 double crochets into the first stitch, followed by a double crochet. Chain 1, skip 1 stitch, and double crochet. Repeat this pattern until you reach the center space. In the center space, work a double crochet, chain 2, and another double crochet. Continue with chain 1, skip 1 stitch, and double crochet until you reach the last stitch, where you'll make 3 double crochets. Turn your work.

Row 12: Chain 3, make 2 double crochets into the first stitch. Double crochet in each stitch and chain space until you reach the center space. In the center space, work a double crochet, chain 2, and another double crochet. Then, double crochet in each stitch and chain space until you reach the last stitch, where you'll make 3 double crochets. Turn your work.

Row 13: Chain 3, make 2 double crochets into the first stitch, followed by a double crochet. Chain 1, skip 1 stitch, and double crochet. Repeat this pattern until you reach the center space. In the center space, work a double crochet, chain 2, and another double crochet. Then, continue with chain 1, skip 1 stitch, and double crochet until you reach the last stitch, where you'll make 3 double crochets. Turn your work.

Row 14: Chain 3, make 2 double crochets into the first stitch, chain 2, and skip 2 stitches. Double crochet, chain 2, skip 2 stitches. Repeat this pattern until you reach the center space. In the center space, work a double crochet, chain 2, and another double crochet. Then, continue with double crochet, chain 2, skip 2 stitches until you reach the last stitch, where you'll make 3 double crochets. Turn your work.

Row 15: Chain 3, make 2 double crochets into the first stitch, followed by a double crochet. Chain 1, skip 1 stitch, and double crochet. Repeat this pattern until you reach the center space. In the center space, work a double crochet, chain 2, and another double crochet. Continue with chain 1, skip 1 stitch, and double crochet until you reach the last stitch, where you'll make 3 double crochets. Turn your work.

Row 16: Chain 1, make 3 single crochets into the first stitch, followed by a single crochet twice more. Then, work a Bobble stitch. Single crochet 3, then work a Bobble stitch. Repeat this pattern until you're one stitch away from the center space. In the center space, make a single crochet, chain 2, and another single crochet. After that, work a Bobble stitch, and repeat single crochet 3, Bobble stitch until you have 3 stitches left. Make 2 single crochets and then 3 single crochets in the last stitch. Turn your work.

Row 17: Chain 3, make 2 double crochets into the first stitch, followed by a double crochet. Chain 1, skip 1 stitch, and double crochet. Repeat this pattern until you reach the center space. In the center space, work a double crochet, chain 2, and another double crochet. After that, continue with chain 1, skip 1 stitch, and double crochet until you reach the last stitch, where you'll make 3 double crochets. Turn your work.

Note: Make sure to place 1 double crochet on top of each Bobble stitch in this row.

Row 18: Chain 3, make 2 double crochets into the first stitch. Double crochet in each stitch and chain space until you reach the center space. In the center space, work a double crochet, chain 2, and another double crochet. Then, double crochet in each stitch and chain space until you reach the last stitch, where you'll make 3 double crochets. Turn your work.

Row 19: Chain 3, make 2 double crochets into the first stitch. Double crochet 53 more times. In the center space, work a double crochet, chain 2, and another double crochet. Continue with double crochets 53 more times, and finish with 3 double crochets in the last stitch. Turn your work.

Row 20: Chain 3, make 2 double crochets into the first stitch, followed by double crocheting 56 more times. In the center space, work a double crochet, chain 2, and another double crochet. Continue with double crochets 56 more times, and end with 3 double crochets in the last stitch. Turn your work.

Row 21: Chain 3, make 2 double crochets into the first stitch, followed by double crocheting 59 more times. In the center space, work a double crochet, chain 2, and another double crochet. Continue with double crochets 59 more times, and finish with 3 double crochets in the last stitch. Turn your work.

Row 22: Chain 3, make 2 double crochets into the first stitch. Double crochet 62 more times. In the center space, work a double crochet, chain 2, and another double crochet. Continue with double crochets 62 more times, and finish with 3 double crochets in the last stitch. Turn your work.

Row 23: Chain 3, make 2 double crochets into the first stitch, followed by double crocheting 65 more times. In the center space, work a double crochet, chain 2, and another double crochet. Continue with double crochets 65 more times, and end with 3 double crochets in the last stitch. Turn your work.

Row 24: Chain 3, make 2 double crochets into the first stitch, followed by double crocheting 68 more times. In the center space, work a double crochet, chain 2, and another double crochet. Continue with double crochets 68 more times, and finish with 3 double crochets in the last stitch. Turn your work.

Row 25: Chain 3, make 2 double crochets into the first stitch. Double crochet 71 more times. In the center space, work a double crochet, chain 2, and another double crochet. Continue with double crochets 71 more times, and finish with 3 double crochets in the last stitch. Turn your work.

Row 26: Chain 3, make 2 double crochets into the first stitch, followed by double crocheting 74 more times. In the center space, work a double crochet, chain 2, and another double crochet. Continue with double crochets 74 more times, and end with 3 double crochets in the last stitch. Turn your work.

Row 27: Chain 3, make 2 double crochets into the first stitch, followed by a double crochet. Chain 1, skip 1 stitch, and double crochet. Repeat this pattern until you reach the center space. In the center space, work a double crochet, chain 2, and another double crochet. After that, continue with chain 1, skip 1 stitch, and double crochet until you reach the last stitch, where you'll make 3 double crochets. Turn your work.

Row 28: Chain 3, make 2 double crochets into the first stitch. Double crochet in each stitch and chain space until you reach the center space. In the center space, work a double crochet, chain 2, and another double crochet. Then, double crochet in each stitch and chain space until you reach the last stitch, where you'll make 3 double crochets. Turn your work.

Row 29: Chain 3, make 2 double crochets into the first stitch, followed by double crocheting 83 more times. In the center space, work a double crochet, chain 2, and another double crochet. Continue with double crochets 83 more times, and end with 3 double crochets in the last stitch. Turn your work.

Row 30: Chain 3, make 2 double crochets into the first stitch, followed by double crocheting 86 more times. In the center space, work a double crochet, chain 2, and another double crochet. Continue with double crochets 86 more times, and finish with 3 double crochets in the last stitch. Turn your work.

Row 31: Chain 3, make 2 double crochets into the first stitch, followed by a double crochet. Chain 1, skip 1 stitch, and double crochet. Repeat this pattern until you reach the center space. In the center space, work a double crochet, chain 2, and another double crochet. After that, continue with chain 1, skip 1 stitch, and double crochet until you reach the last stitch, where you'll make 3 double crochets. Turn your work.

Row 32: Chain 3, make 2 double crochets into the first stitch. Double crochet in each stitch and chain space until you reach the center space. In the center space, work a double crochet, chain 2, and another double crochet. Then, double crochet in each stitch and chain space until you reach the last stitch, where you'll make 3 double crochets. Turn your work.

Row 33: Chain 3, make 2 double crochets into the first stitch, followed by a double crochet. Chain 1, skip 1 stitch, and double crochet. Repeat this pattern until you reach the center space. In the center space, work a double crochet, chain 2, and another double crochet. After that, continue with chain 1, skip 1 stitch, and double crochet until you reach the last stitch, where you'll make 3 double crochets. Turn your work.

Row 34: Chain 3, make 2 double crochets into the first stitch. Chain 2, skip 2 stitches, and then double crochet, chain 2, skip 2 stitches. Repeat this pattern until you reach the center space. In the center space, work a double crochet, chain 2, and another double crochet. Continue with chain 2, skip 2 stitches, double crochet, chain 2, skip 2 stitches until you reach the last stitch, where you'll make 3 double crochets. Turn your work.

Row 35: Chain 3, make 2 double crochets into the first stitch, followed by a double crochet. Chain 1, skip 1 stitch, and double crochet. Repeat this pattern until you reach the center space. In the center space, work a double crochet, chain 2, and another double crochet. After that, continue with chain 1, skip 1 stitch, and double crochet until you reach the last stitch, where you'll make 3 double crochets. Turn your work.

Row 36: Chain 1, make 3 single crochets into the first stitch. Single crochet 2 more times. Then, work a bobble stitch, single crochet 3 times, and a bobble stitch. Repeat this pattern until you're one stitch before the center space. In the center space, make a single crochet, chain 2, and another single crochet. After that, continue with bobble stitch, single crochet 3 times, and a bobble stitch until you're left with 3 stitches. Single crochet 2 times, and then make 3 single crochets in the last stitch. Turn your work.

Row 37: Chain 3, make 2 double crochets into the first stitch, followed by a double crochet. Chain 1, skip 1 stitch, and double crochet. Repeat this pattern until you reach the center space. In the center space, work a double crochet, chain 2, and another double crochet. After that, continue with chain 1, skip 1 stitch, and double crochet until you reach the last stitch. Make sure to place 1 double crochet on top of each bobble stitch, then finish with 3 double crochets in the last stitch. Turn your work.

Row 38: Chain 3, make 2 double crochets into the first stitch. Double crochet in each stitch and chain space until you reach the center space. In the center space, work a double crochet, chain 2, and another double crochet. Then, double crochet in each stitch and chain space until you reach the last stitch, where you'll make 3 double crochets. Turn your work.

Row 39: Chain 3, make 2 double crochets into the first stitch, followed by double crocheting 113 more times. In the center space, work a double crochet, chain 2, and another double crochet. Continue with double crochets 113 more times, and end with 3 double crochets in the last stitch. Turn your work.

Row 40: Chain 3, make 2 double crochets into the first stitch, followed by double crocheting 116 more times. In the center space, work a double crochet, chain 2, and another double crochet. Continue with double crochets 116 more times, and finish with 3 double crochets in the last stitch. Turn your work.

Row 41: Chain 3, make 2 double crochets into the first stitch, followed by double crocheting 119 more times. In the center space, work a double crochet, chain 2, and another double crochet. Continue with double crochets 109 more times, and end with 3 double crochets in the last stitch. Turn your work.

Row 42: Chain 3, make 2 double crochets into the first stitch, followed by double crocheting 122 more times. In the center space, work a double crochet, chain 2, and another double crochet. Continue with double crochets 122 more times, and finish with 3 double crochets in the last stitch. Turn your work.

Row 43: Chain 3, make 2 double crochets into the first stitch, followed by double crocheting 125 more times. In the center space, work a double crochet, chain 2, and another double crochet. Continue with double crochets 125 more times, and finish with 3 double crochets in the last stitch. Turn your work.

Row 44: Chain 3, make 2 double crochets into the first stitch, followed by double crocheting 128 more times. In the center space, work a double crochet, chain 2, and another double crochet. Continue with double crochets 128 more times, and end with 3 double crochets in the last stitch. Turn your work.

Row 45: Chain 3, make 2 double crochets into the first stitch, followed by double crocheting 131 more times. In the center space, work a double crochet, chain 2, and another double crochet. Continue with double crochets 131 more times. There is no need to turn your work at the end of Row 45.

Fasten off.

Weave in all of your ends. Steam and block your wrap.

Sweater

- Yarn
- 6mm (US J) Crochet Hook
- Darning Needle
- Scissors
- St markers

Measurements cm:

Bust: 92

Length: 56

Armhole: 16

Sleeve length: 41

Terms:

Ch = Chain

Sl st = Slip Stitch

SC = Single Crochet

SC2tog = Sc 2 stitches together

BLO = Back Loop

St(s) = Stitch(es)

Rep = Repeat

Sk = Skip

GAUGE: 10cm/4" square = 15 stitches wide x 16 rows tall in sc column stitch

Instructions

Sc Columns:

Chain an even number of chains.

Row 1: Single crochet in the second chain from the hook, chain 1, skip 1, single crochet; repeat from * to * until the end of the row. Turn your work.

Row 2: Chain 1, single crochet in the first stitch, chain 1, skip 1, single crochet; repeat from * to * until the end of the row. Turn your work.

Repeat Row 2 until you reach the desired length.

Back panel

From the bottom up, body panels are crocheted. The back panel is made by crocheting along the ribbing's long edge after it has been worked vertically.

Back ribbing

Foundation chain: ch 9.

Row 1: Single crochet into the second chain from the hook, and single crochet in each stitch until the end of the row. Turn your work. (8 stitches)

Row 2: Chain 1, single crochet in the back loop only (BLO) for the first 7 stitches, and single crochet in the last stitch. Turn your work. (8 stitches)

Repeat Row 2 until you reach Row 69.

Don't loosen up! Now, we'll work along the band's long edge. One St is equivalent to each row.

Back

Row 1: Chain 1, single crochet in the first row, chain 1, skip 1 row, single crochet in the next row; repeat from * to * until the end of the row. Turn your work. (69 stitches)

Row 2: Chain 1, single crochet in the first stitch, chain 1, skip 1 stitch, single crochet; repeat from * to * until the end of the row. Turn your work. (69 stitches)

Repeat Row 2 until you reach Row 80.

 Note: You can add or remove rows to make your sweater longer or shorter.

FRONT PANEL

Repeat 'BACK PANEL' instructions until ROW 70.

If you changed the back panel's length, continue crocheting until you are 10 rows short of the total number of rows in the panel. For example, if you worked 54 rows to make the rear panel, work 44 rows to make the front panel.

Don't loosen up! Now we'll crochet the shape for the shoulders.

Shoulder shaping

Counting from your crochet hook, place a St marker in the 28th st.

*The St marker should be in a chain space, not a SC.

Row 1: Chain 1, single crochet in the first stitch, chain 1, skip 1 stitch, single crochet; repeat from * to * until you have 2 stitches left before the stitch marker, then single crochet the last 2 stitches together (SC2tog). Turn your work. (26 stitches)

Row 2: Chain 1, single crochet the first 2 stitches together (SC2tog), chain 1, skip 1 stitch, single crochet; repeat from * to * until the end of the row. Turn your work. (25 stitches)

Row 3: Chain 1, single crochet in the first stitch, chain 1, skip 1 stitch, single crochet; repeat from * to * until you have 2 stitches left, then single crochet the last 2 stitches together (SC2tog). Turn your work. (24 stitches)

Row 4: Repeat Row 2. (23 stitches)

Row 5: Repeat Row 3. (22 stitches)

Row 6: Repeat Row 2. (21 stitches)

Row 7: Repeat Row 3. (20 stitches)

Row 8: Repeat Row 2. (19 stitches)

Row 9: Chain 1, single crochet in the first stitch, chain 1, skip 1 stitch, single crochet; repeat from * to * until the end. Ensure that the last single crochet is made on top of the previous SC2tog from Row 6. Turn your work. (19 stitches)

Row 10: Chain 1, single crochet in the first stitch, chain 1, skip 1 stitch, single crochet; repeat from * to * until the end. Fasten off and turn. (19 stitches)

Counting from the St marker, skip 14 sts, insert hook into next st (hook should be in a SC) and pull up a loop.

Row 1: Chain 1, single crochet 2 together (SC2tog), single crochet (SC), chain 1, skip 1 stitch, single crochet; repeat from * to * until the end. Turn. (26 stitches)

You can place a stitch marker into the SC2tog to make it easier to find. In Row 2, the SC2tog is the last stitch of the row.

Row 2: Chain 1, single crochet (SC), chain 1, skip 1 stitch; repeat from * to * until 2 stitches are left, SC2tog, turn. (25 stitches)

Row 3: Chain 1, single crochet 2 together (SC2tog), single crochet (SC), chain 1, skip 1 stitch, single crochet; repeat from * to * until the end. Turn. (24 stitches)

If using the stitch marker, place it in the single crochet 2 together.

Row 4: Repeat Row 2. (23 stitches)

Row 5: Repeat Row 3. (22 stitches)

Row 6: Repeat Row 2. (21 stitches)

Row 7: Repeat Row 3. (20 stitches)

Row 8: Repeat Row 2. (19 stitches)

Row 9: Ch 1, SC (first SC should be on top of the SC2tog), *ch 1, sk 1 st, SC; rep from * until end, turn. (19 stitches)

Row 10: Ch 1, SC, *ch 1, sk 1 st, SC; rep from * until end. Fasten off. (19 stitches)

Sleeves

(make 2)

Working from the cuff up, the sleeves are done. Just as with the body panels, we'll chain the ribbing in a vertical fashion before chaining the sleeve right on to the edge.

Sleeve ribbing

Foundation chain: ch 11.

Row 1: SC into the 2nd chain from the hook, SC in each stitch until the end, and then turn. (10 stitches)

Row 2: Ch 1, BLO SC 9, SC in the last stitch, and then turn. (10 stitches)

repeat Row 2 until you reach Row 31.

Don't loosen up! Now let's crochet along the band's long edge.

Sleeve

Row 1: Ch 1, SC, ch 1, sk 1, SC across until the end, and then turn. (31 stitches)

Rows 2 - 4: Ch 1, SC, ch 1, sk 1, SC across until the end, and then turn. (31 stitches for each of these rows)

Row 5: Ch 1, 2SC in the 1st st, SC, ch 1, sk 1 across until the last st, 2SC in the last st, and then turn. (33 stitches)

Rows 6 - 8: Ch 1, SC, ch 1, sk 1, SC across until the last st, SC in the last st, and then turn. (33 stitches)

Row 9: Ch 1, SC, ch 1, SC across, and then turn. (35 stitches)

Rows 10 - 13: Repeat stitch on ROWS 2 - 4. (35 stitches for each of these rows)

Row 14: Repeat ROW 5. (37 stitches)

Rows 15 - 17: Rep ROWS 6 - 8. (37 stitches for each of these rows)

Row 18: Rep ROW 9. (39 stitches)

Rows 19 - 22: Rep ROWS 2 - 4. (39 stitches for each of these rows)

Row 23: Rep ROW 5. (41 stitches)

Rows 24 - 26: Rep ROWS 6 - 8. (41 stitches for each of these rows)

Row 27: Rep ROW 9. (43 stitches)

Rows 28 - 31: Rep ROWS 2 - 4. (43 stitches for each of these rows)

Row 32: Rep ROW 5. (45 stitches)

Rows 33 - 35: Rep ROWS 6 - 8. (49 stitches for each of these rows)

Row 36: Rep ROW 9. (51 stitches)

Rows 37 - 40: Rep ROWS 2 - 4. (51 stitches for each of these rows)

Row 41: Rep ROW 5. (53 stitches)

Rows 42 - 44: Repeat ROWS 6 - 8. (53 stitches for each of these rows)

Row 45: Repeat ROW 9. (55 stitches)

Rows 46 - 49: Repeat ROWS 2 - 4. (55 stitches for each of these rows)

Row 50: Repeat ROW 5. (57 stitches)

Rows 51 - 53: Repeat ROWS 6 - 8. (53 stitches for each of these rows)

Row 54: Repeat ROW 9. (55 stitches)

Fasten off.

Fold sleeve in half lengthways and whip St sides together.

Neckline ribbing

Foundation chain: ch 6.

Row 1: Single crochet into the second chain from the hook, and single crochet in each stitch until the end of the row. Turn your work. (5 stitches)

Row 2: Chain 1, single crochet in the back loop only (BLO) for the first 4 stitches, and single crochet in the last stitch. Turn your work. (5 stitches)

Repeat Row 2 until the ribbing measures 46cm/18" or approximately for 66 rows.

Assembly

Stack the front and rear panels one on top of the other.

Sew shoulder seams together using whip stitching.

Whip St up the sides of body panels together, leaving a 16 cm/ 6.5 gap for the sleeves.

*Sew from the top of the ribbing if you would want a split at the side seam, as seen in the photo. Start sewing at the bottom of the ribbing if you want to avoid a split.

The sleeves' tops should be whip-stitched to the body.

Evenly whip St the neckline ribbing across the exposed neckline edge.

Sew the neckline ribbing's edges together.

Sew the neckline ribbing's edges together.

Bring all of your ends together.

Your sweater will block and steam.

That's it.

BOOK 3:
STEP-BY-STEP PROJECTS FOR INTERMEDIATE

SNAIL BLANKET

Crochet this adorable snail blanket; it's excellent for any house and will provide comfort throughout the year. Using basic crochet stitches, create this snail blanket in a color that best suits the recipient.

What you need?

- 5mm Crochet Hook
- yarns
- Parchment – 1070 yards
- White – 80 yards
- Teal – 40 yards
- Scissors
- Tapestry Needle – Weaving in ends
- Tape Measure
- Size 38 x 37.25 inches approx

Terms:

Slip Stitch

Ch – Chain

Sc – Single Crochet

Dc – Double Crochet

Sts – Stitches

Sk – Skip

Turn your blanket over at the end of each row. This crochet design is done in rows, starting at the bottom and working your way up.

Throughout the design, the first ch1 at the beginning of each row does not count as a stitch.

Every row will have 147 stitches at the end, which consists of all dc and ch threads. If you are receiving a different St count, it is likely that you missed a ch1 St on either your previous or current row.

The stitches you are working into might be chain 1 stitches or dc stitches, for example, when the design instructs you to work "1dc in the following 12sts."

All you are doing when the pattern says "ch1, sk1" is chaining one and skipping the subsequent stitch, which might be a chain one or a dc stitch.

First, crochet the contents in the brackets. Then, once the bracket closes, continue crocheting the contents in the brackets as many times as directed. This would apply, for example, if the row you are working on has brackets. (Ch1, sk1, 1dc in next st).

Till the round's conclusion, repeat the information between the stars from * to *.

If your row contains a **, you must continue to work the pattern from * to * throughout the length of the row. As the row approaches its completion, you will finish the final repeat at ** as you are no longer able to work the whole repeat. Then, proceed as directed to finish the row.

Instruction

Row 1: Chain 148, work 1 double crochet (dc) in the 2nd chain from the hook and in each chain across, then turn. (147 dc)

Row 2: Chain 1, work 1 dc in each stitch across, and turn. (147 dc)

Row 3: Chain 1, work 1 dc in the first 16 stitches. [(Chain 1, skip 1 stitch, work 1 dc in the next stitch)] - Repeat 8 more times. Then, work 1 dc in the next 29 stitches. Repeat from * to * all the way across the row until 19 stitches remain, finishing the last repeat at **. Finally, work 1 dc in the last 19 stitches, and turn. (147 sts)

Row 4: Chain 1, work 1 dc in the first 18 stitches. [(Chain 1, skip 1 stitch, work 1 dc in the next 17 stitches), (chain 1, skip 1 stitch, work 1 dc in the next stitch)] - Repeat 2 more times. Then, work 1 dc in the next 23 stitches. Repeat from * to * all the way across the row until 11 stitches remain, finishing the last repeat at **. Finally, work 1 dc in the last 11 stitches, and turn. (147 stitches)

Row 5: Chain 1, work 1 dc in the first 10 stitches. [(Chain 1, skip 1 stitch, work 1 dc in the next 7 stitches), (chain 1, skip 1 stitch, work 1 dc in the next 17 stitches), (chain 1, skip 1 stitch)] - Repeat 2 more times. Then, work 1 dc in the next 20 stitches. Repeat from * to * all the way across the row until 16 stitches remain, finishing the last repeat at **. Finally, work 1 dc in the last 16 stitches, and turn. (147 stitches)

Row 6: Chain 1, work 1 dc in the first 16 stitches. [(Chain 1, skip 1 stitch, work 1 dc in the next 15 stitches), (chain 1, skip 1 stitch, work 1 dc in the next 11 stitches), (chain 1, skip 1 stitch)] - Repeat 2 more times. Then, work 1 dc in the next 18 stitches. Repeat from * to * all the way across the row until 8 stitches remain, finishing the last repeat at **. Finally, work 1 dc in the last 8 stitches, and turn. (147 stitches)

Row 7: Chain 1, work 1 dc in the first 7 stitches. [(Chain 1, skip 1 stitch, work 1 dc in the next 8 stitches), (chain 1, skip 1 stitch, work 1 dc in the next stitch)] - Repeat 4 more times. Then, work 1 dc in the next 12 stitches. Repeat from * to * all the way across the row until 14 stitches remain, finishing the last repeat at **. Finally, work 1 dc in the last 14 stitches, and turn. (147 stitches)

Row 8: Chain 1, work 1 dc in the first 10 stitches. [(Chain 1, skip 1 stitch, work 1 dc in the next stitch), (chain 1, skip 1 stitch)] - Repeat 1 more time. Then, work 1 dc in the next 12 stitches. After that, chain 1, skip 1, and work 1 dc in the next 11 stitches. Then, chain 1, skip 1, and work 1 dc in the next 7 stitches. Finally, chain 1, skip 1, and work 1 dc in the last 6 stitches, and turn. (147 stitches)

Row 9: Chain 1, work 1 dc in the first 6 stitches. *[(Chain 1, skip 1 stitch, work 1 dc in the next 6 stitches), (chain 1, skip 1 stitch, work 1 dc in the next 14 stitches), (chain 1, skip 1 stitch, work 1 dc in the next 15 stitches), (chain 1, skip 1 stitch, work 1 dc in the next 8 stitches)] - Repeat from * to * all the way across the row, and turn. (147 stitches)

Row 10: Chain 1, work 1 dc in the first 6 stitches. [(Chain 1, skip 1 stitch, work 1 dc in the next 16 stitches), (chain 1, skip 1 stitch, work 1 dc in the next 6 stitches), (chain 1, skip 1 stitch, work 1 dc in the next stitch)] - Repeat 2 more times. Then, work 1 dc in the next 4 stitches. Next, chain 1, skip 1, and work 1 dc in the next 5 stitches. After that, chain 1, skip 1, and work 1 dc in the next 6 stitches. Repeat from * to * all the way across the row, and turn. (147 stitches)

Row 11: Chain 1, work 1 dc in the first 6 stitches. [(Chain 1, skip 1 stitch, work 1 dc in the next 5 stitches), (chain 1, skip 1 stitch, work 1 dc in the next 4 stitches), (chain 1, skip 1 stitch, work 1 dc in the next 6 stitches), (chain 1, skip 1 stitch, work 1 dc in the next 5 stitches), (chain 1, skip 1 stitch, work 1 dc in the next stitch)] - Repeat 1 more time. Then, work 1 dc in the next 12 stitches. Afterward, chain 1, skip 1, and work 1 dc in the next 6 stitches. Repeat from * to * all the way across the row, and turn. (147 stitches)

Row 12: Chain 1, work 1 dc in the first 6 stitches. [(Chain 1, skip 1 stitch), (1 dc in the next 5 stitches, chain 1, skip 1 stitch)] - Repeat 1 more time. Then, work 1 dc in the next 3 stitches. Next, chain 1, skip 1, and work 1 dc in the next 5 stitches. After that, chain 1, skip 1, and work 1 dc in the next 3 stitches. Then, [(chain 1, skip 1 stitch, work 1 dc in the next stitch)] - Repeat 1 more time. Finally, work 1 dc in the next 3 stitches, chain 1, skip 1, and work 1 dc in the next 6 stitches. Repeat from * to * all the way across the row, and turn. (147 stitches)

Row 13: Chain 1, work 1 dc in the first 6 stitches. *[(Chain 1, skip 1 stitch, work 1 dc in the next 7 stitches), (chain 1, skip 1 stitch, work 1 dc in the next 8 stitches), (chain 1, skip 1 stitch, work 1 dc in the next 6 stitches), (chain 1, skip 1 stitch, work 1 dc in the next 3 stitches), (chain 1, skip 1 stitch, work 1 dc in the next 9 stitches), (chain 1, skip 1 stitch, work 1 dc in the next 8 stitches)] - Repeat from * to * all the way across the row, and turn. (147 stitches)

Row 14: Chain 1, work 1 dc in the first 10 stitches. *[(Chain 1, skip 1 stitch), (1 dc in the next stitch) - Repeat 3 more times, (1 dc in the next 5 stitches), (chain 1, skip 1 stitch, work 1 dc in the next 6 stitches), (chain 1, skip 1 stitch)] - Repeat 3 more times. Then, work 1 dc in the next 7 stitches. After that, chain 1, skip 1, and work 1 dc in the next 11 stitches. Repeat from * to * all the way across the row, and turn. (147 stitches)

Row 15: Chain 1, work 1 dc in the first 8 stitches. *[(Chain 1, skip 1 stitch, work 1 dc in the next 19 stitches), (chain 1, skip 1 stitch, work 1 dc in the next 7 stitches), (chain 1, skip 1 stitch, work 1 dc in the next 5 stitches), (chain 1, skip 1 stitch)] - Repeat until there are 10 stitches left, finishing the last repeat at the last 10 stitches. Turn. (147 stitches)

Row 16: Chain 1, work 1 dc in the first 10 stitches. *[(Chain 1, skip 1 stitch, work 1 dc in the next 5 stitches), (chain 1, skip 1 stitch, work 1 dc in the next 9 stitches), (chain 1, skip 1 stitch, work 1 dc in the next 15 stitches), (chain 1, skip 1 stitch)] - Repeat until there are 10 stitches left, finishing the last repeat at the last 10 stitches. Turn. (147 stitches)

Row 17: Chain 1, work 1 dc in the first 12 stitches. *[(Chain 1, skip 1 stitch), (1 dc in the next stitch) - Repeat 6 more times, (1 dc in the next 12 stitches), (chain 1, skip 1 stitch, work 1 dc in the next 5 stitches), (chain 1, skip 1 stitch)] - Repeat until there are 8 stitches left, finishing the last repeat at the last 8 stitches. Turn. (147 stitches)

Rows 18-19: Chain 1, work 1 dc in each stitch across, and turn. (147 dc)

Repeat rows 3-19 until blanket measures 36.25 inches approx finishing on row 19 – Fasten off – Move on to border.

Border:

Row 1: In the upper right corner, join the white yarn. Work 1 single crochet (sc) evenly around the blanket, working 1 sc, chain 2 (ch2), 1 sc into each corner. Join with a slip stitch (slip st) to begin the next row of sc.

Row 2: Work (1 sc, ch2, 1 sc) into each ch2 corner space around the blanket, joining with a slip stitch (slip st) to begin the next sc.

We utilize a DK yarn for the following row, but I had to be careful not to crochet it too tightly because it was a thinner yarn and would have puckered the blanket.

Row 3: Join teal yarn in any stitch, work 1sc evenly around the entire blanket, working (1sc, ch1, 1sc) into each corner of the blanket, join with a slip St to beg sc.

Securely fasten and tuck in all ends.

ICE CREAM CONE

What you need?

- Hobbii 8/6 Cotton 03 & 09
- Crochet Hook E-4 3.5 mm
- Yarn Needle
- Scissors
- Measuring Tape

Terms:

Sc = sc

Chain = ch

Half Double Crochet = hdc

Double Crochet = dc

Slip St = sl st

Sizing

The finished ice cream measures 2 inches by 2 inches at its widest points.

The cone's final dimensions are 2.5 inches high by 2.5 inches broad at its widest points.

Changing the yarn or weight of the yarn might affect the final size.

Instruction

Ice Cream

Row 1: Chain 3 (this is your first double crochet). In the third chain from the hook, work 7 double crochets (dc) in the same stitch. This creates a group of 8 double crochets in total.

Then, turn your work.

Row 2: Chain 3 (this is your first double crochet). In the first stitch, work 1 double crochet (dc).

Now, you'll create an increase by repeating this pattern: double crochet 2 times (dc 2x) into the next stitch. Do this until you've worked a total of 16 stitches.

Finally, turn your work.

Row 3: Chain 1 (this is your first single crochet). Work 7 single crochets (sc) evenly across the bottom of the first row. This means you'll place 1 single crochet in each of the 8 stitches from the previous row.

Then, turn your work.

Row 4: Chain 1. Work 1 single crochet (sc) into each of the 8 stitches across. You should have 8 sc stitches at the end of this row.

Row 5: Chain 1. In the first stitch, work the following stitches: 1 half double crochet (hdc), 1 double crochet (dc), 1 hdc, 1 hdc. Slip stitch (sl st) into the next stitch. Work 2 double crochets (2 dc) into the next stitch.

Work 1 single crochet (sc) into the next stitch.

In the next stitch, work 1 double crochet (dc), 1 double crochet (dc), 1 half double crochet (hdc).

Slip stitch (sl st) into the next stitch.

Work 1 single crochet (sc) into the next stitch.

Finally, work 3 double crochets (3 dc) into the last stitch.

To Finish:

Slip stitch (sl st) into the first stitch of row 2.

Work slip stitches (sl st) around the piece.

End with a total of 17 slip stitches (sl st).

The final slip stitch should be placed in the first stitch of row 5.

Cone

Row 1: Chain 2. Work 1 single crochet (sc) into the first stitch. Turn your work. You should have 1 sc in this row.

Row 2: Chain 1. Work 1 sc increase (sc inc). Turn your work. You should have 2 sc stitches in this row.

Row 3: Chain 1. Work 1 sc increase (sc inc). Work 1 single crochet (sc) into the next stitch. Turn your work. You should have 3 sc stitches in this row.

Row 4: Chain 1. Work 1 sc increase (sc inc). Work 1 single crochet (sc) into each of the next 2 stitches.

Turn your work. You should have 4 sc stitches in this row.

Row 5: Chain 1. Work 1 sc increase (sc inc). Work 1 single crochet (sc) into each of the next 3 stitches.

Turn your work. You should have 5 sc stitches in this row.

Row 6: Chain 1. Work 1 single crochet (sc) into each stitch across. Turn your work. You should have 5 sc stitches in this row.

Row 7: Chain 1. Work 1 sc increase (sc inc). Work 1 single crochet (sc) into each of the next 4 stitches.

Turn your work. You should have 6 sc stitches in this row.

Row 8: Chain 1. Work 1 single crochet (sc) into each stitch across. Turn your work. You should have 6 sc stitches in this row.

Row 9: Chain 1. Work 1 sc increase (sc inc). Work 1 single crochet (sc) into each of the next 5 stitches. Turn your work. You should have 7 sc stitches in this row.

Row 10: Chain 1. Work 1 single crochet (sc) into each stitch across. Turn your work. You should have 7 sc stitches in this row.

Row 11: Chain 1. Work 1 sc increase (sc inc). Work 1 single crochet (sc) into each of the next 6 stitches.

Turn your work. You should have 8 sc stitches in this row.

Row 12: Chain 1. Work 1 slip stitch (sl st) into each stitch across. You should have 8 sl st stitches in this row.

Finishing: Work more sl sts around the cone's perimeter before cutting the yarn, leaving a 4-inch tail for sewing the cone and ice cream together.

If you'd like, you can ch 1 at the corners and the point before moving on to the next sl st.

Join the cone and the ice cream.

Turn the ice cream and cone over so that the cone is on top of the ice cream.

Join the ice cream and cone by tying the yarn needle onto the 4-inch yarn tail. Similar to how the ice cream is not required to be straight, neither is the cone.

After attaching the cone and ice cream, you can use scissors to cut off the excess and weave in the remaining loose ends of the cone.

Colorful Baby Blanket

Size: 24-inches wide X 36- inches long

Gauge: 17 Stitches every 4-inches. 13 rows every 4-inches.

What you need?

- Red 4 skeins or 1,080 yards. I used about half of the last skein.
- Hook Size J, 6 MM
- Yarn Needle
- Scissors

Terms:

CH = Chain

SC = Single Crochet

SP = Space

ST = Stitch

STs = Stitches

[ ] = Repeat

The foundation Ch St is stitched in multiples of two even stitches.

In the second chain from the hook, the first St is worked.

Instead of working the last chain 1 in the final sc three together, work a sc in the previous St that you worked.

Row 2 is repeated until you achieve the required size in this design.

Make an effort to use slightly looser stitches. You will be able to hook into the stitches in the preceding row more easily as a result.

At the end of every row, turn.

Instruction

Starting Chain 100

Row 1: SC in the second CH after hooking up. Pull up a loop by inserting the hook into the same SP as the SC ST. Toggle a loop for the next two steps. At this stage, your hook ought to have four loops. Pull through each of the four loops on your hook, YO. To finish this stitch, CH 1. [Pull up a loop in the next two STs, YO and pull through all four loops on the hook, then close with CH 1 after inserting the hook into the same SP]. Continue from [ ] across. concludes the row. Instead of concluding with the Ch 1 in the last ST, work on a SC. Turn it.

Row 2: As you worked the CH 1 (the first ST), you also worked the CH 1, SC. Pull up a loop by inserting the hook into the same SP as the SC ST. Toggle a loop for the next two steps. At this stage, your hook ought to have four loops. Pull through each of the four loops on your hook, YO. To finish this stitch, CH 1. [Pull up a loop in the next two STs, YO and pull through all four loops on the hook, then close with CH 1 after inserting the hook into the same SP]. Repeat between [ ] across. In the last ST, do not close with the Ch 1, rather work a SC in the last ST. Turn

Rows 3-116: Repeat row 2.

Rounding up.

After working in a chain stitch, cut the yarn, leaving a tail of about 12 inches. Pull the yarn snugly after threading it through the chain stitch. After cutting out extra yarn, weave in the yarn tail with the yarn needle..

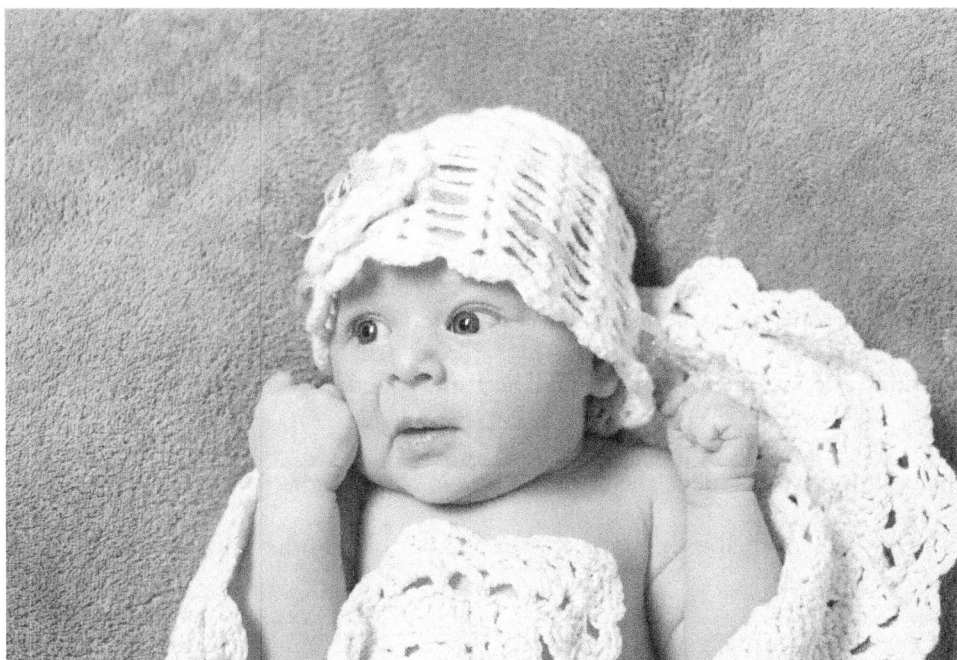

CROP TOP

The size: 14 stitches /12 rows = 10 cm/4 inches in Hdc

At the start of the row, Ch 2 does not count as a stitch.

Stitches are counted for chain stitches.

Bottom up work is done on the pattern.

What you need?

- weight yarn -1 balls of 100g
- 4.0 mm crochet hook
- St markers
- Scissors

Terms:

Ch: Chain

Hdc: Half double crochet

HdcCS: Half double crochet Cross Stitch

Skip the next Hdc , Hdc in the next stitch, then Hdc in the skipped Hdc.

Hdc2tog: Half double crochet two together

Sc: Single Crochet

Slst: Slip stitch

* * or **: repeat the instructions between the asterisk

Instruction

Ch 85

Row 1: Make half-double crochet (Hdc) stitches in each of the first 83 chains. (83 Hdc)

Row 2: Chain 2 and turn your work. Make an Hdc in the first stitch and the next 5 stitches. Then, chain 1, skip 1 stitch, make a Hdc cluster stitch (HdcCS), chain 1, skip 1 stitch, make 12 Hdc stitches. Repeat this pattern until you reach the end of the row, finishing with 9 Hdc stitches. (83 stitches)

Row 3: Chain 2 and turn your work. Make Hdc stitches in each stitch across. (83 stitches)

Row 4: Chain 2 and turn your work. Make an Hdc in the first stitch and the next 12 stitches. Then, chain 1, skip 1 stitch, make a Hdc cluster stitch (HdcCS), chain 1, skip 1 stitch, make 12 Hdc stitches. Repeat this pattern until you reach the end of the row, finishing with 2 Hdc stitches. (83 stitches)

Row 5: Repeat row 3, which means you should make Hdc stitches in each stitch across. (83 stitches)

Row 6: Chain 2 and turn your work. Make an Hdc in the first stitch and the next 5 stitches. Then, chain 1, skip 1 stitch, make a Hdc cluster stitch (HdcCS), chain 1, skip 1 stitch, make 12 Hdc stitches. Repeat this pattern until you reach the end of the row, finishing with 9 Hdc stitches. (83 stitches)

Row 7: Repeat row 3, which means you should make Hdc stitches in each stitch across. (83 stitches)

Row 8: Chain 2 and turn your work. Make an Hdc in the first stitch and the next 12 stitches. Then, chain 1, skip 1 stitch, make a Hdc cluster stitch (HdcCS), chain 1, skip 1 stitch, make 12 Hdc stitches. Repeat this pattern until you reach the end of the row, finishing with 2 Hdc stitches. (83 stitches)

Row 9: Chain 2 and turn your work. Make a Hdc2tog (Hdc decrease), followed by an Hdc in each stitch across. Finish the row with another Hdc2tog. (81 stitches)

Row 10: Chain 2 and turn your work. Make an Hdc2tog (Hdc decrease), followed by an Hdc in the next 3 stitches. Then, chain 1, skip 1 stitch, make an Hdc cluster stitch (HdcCS), chain 1, skip 1 stitch, make 12 Hdc stitches. Repeat this pattern until you reach the end of the row, finishing with 6 Hdc stitches and an Hdc2tog. (79 stitches)

Row 11: Chain 2 and turn your work. Make an Hdc2tog, followed by an Hdc in each stitch across. Finish the row with another Hdc2tog. (77 stitches)

Row 12: Chain 2 and turn your work. Make an Hdc2tog, followed by an Hdc in the next 8 stitches. Then, chain 1, skip 1 stitch, make an Hdc cluster stitch (HdcCS), chain 1, skip 1 stitch, make 12 Hdc stitches. Repeat this pattern until you reach the end of the row, finishing with 13 Hdc stitches and an Hdc2tog. (75 stitches)

Row 13: Chain 2 and turn your work. Make an Hdc2tog, followed by an Hdc in each stitch across. Finish the row with another Hdc2tog. (73 stitches)

Row 14: Chain 2 and turn your work. Make an Hdc2tog, followed by an Hdc in the next 15 stitches. Then, chain 1, skip 1 stitch, make an Hdc cluster stitch (HdcCS), chain 1, skip 1 stitch, make 12 Hdc stitches. Repeat this pattern until you reach the end of the row, finishing with 2 Hdc stitches and an Hdc2tog. (71 stitches)

Row 15: Chain 2 and turn your work. Make an Hdc2tog, followed by an Hdc in each stitch across. Finish the row with another Hdc2tog. (69 stitches)

Row 16: Chain 2 and turn your work. Make an Hdc2tog, followed by an Hdc in the next 4 stitches. Then, chain 1, skip 1 stitch, make an Hdc cluster stitch (HdcCS), chain 1, skip 1 stitch, make 12 Hdc stitches. Repeat this pattern until you reach the end of the row, finishing with 9 Hdc stitches and an Hdc2tog. (67 stitches)

Heart

Row 17: Chain 2 and turn your work. Make an Hdc2tog, followed by an Hdc in the next 32 stitches. (33 stitches)

Row 18: Without chaining 2, turn your work. Make an Hdc2tog, Hdc in the next 10 stitches, then chain 1, skip 1, make an Hdc cluster stitch (HdcCS), chain 1, skip 1, Hdc in the next 15 stitches, and finally, make an Hdc2tog. (31 stitches)

Row 19: Chain 2 and turn your work. Make an Hdc2tog, and Hdc in each stitch across. Finish the row with an Hdc2tog. (29 stitches)

Row 20: Without chaining 2, turn your work. Make an Hdc2tog, then chain 1, skip 1, make an Hdc cluster stitch (HdcCS), chain 1, skip 1, Hdc in the next 12 stitches, chain 1, skip 1, make another HdcCS, chain 1, skip 1, Hdc in the last 5 stitches, and finish the row with an Hdc2tog. (27 stitches)

Row 21: Repeat row 19. Chain 2 and turn your work, then make an Hdc2tog, Hdc in each stitch across, and finish the row with an Hdc2tog. (25 stitches)

Row 22: Without chaining 2, turn your work. Make an Hdc2tog, Hdc in the next 6 stitches, chain 1, skip 1, make an HdcCS, chain 1, skip 1, Hdc in the next 11 stitches, and finally, make an Hdc2tog. (23 stitches)

Row 23: Repeat row 19 (21 stitches).

Row 24: Without chaining 2, turn your work. Make an Hdc2tog, Hdc in the next 12 stitches, then chain 1, skip 1, make an HdcCS, chain 1, skip 1, Hdc in the next stitch, and finally, make an Hdc2tog. (19 stitches)

Row 25: Repeat row 19 (17 stitches).

Row 26: Without chaining 2, turn your work. Make an Hdc2tog, Hdc in the next 2 stitches, then chain 1, skip 1, make an HdcCS, chain 1, skip 1, Hdc in the next 7 stitches, and finally, make an Hdc2tog. (15 stitches)

Row 27: Chain 2, turn. Make Hdc2tog twice, Hdc in each stitch across, and make 2 Hdc in the last stitch. (14 stitches)

Row 28: Without chaining 2, turn your work. Start with 2 Hdc into the first stitch, then make Hdc in each stitch across, and finish the row with Hdc2tog twice. (13 stitches)

Row 29: Repeat row 27, chain 1, and cut the yarn. (12 stitches).

Reattach yarn with a Slst to the other part of the top at the edge and work towards the middle.

Row 17: Chain 2, Hdc2tog, and Hdc in the next 32 stitches. The last stitch should be worked into the same stitch as the last stitch from the previous Row 17. (33 stitches)

Row 18: Without chaining 2, turn your work. Begin with Hdc2tog, Hdc in the next 14 stitches. Then, Ch 1, skip 1, HdcCS, Ch 1, skip 1, and Hdc in the next 11 stitches. End the row with Hdc2tog. (31 stitches)

Row 19: Chain 2, turn. Start with Hdc2tog, and then make Hdc in each stitch across. Finish the row with Hdc2tog. (29 stitches)

Row 20: Without chaining 2, turn your work. Begin with Hdc2tog, then make Hdc in the next 4 stitches. Continue with Ch 1, skip 1, HdcCS, Ch 1, skip 1, Hdc in 12 stitches, Ch 1, skip 1, HdcCS, Ch 1, skip 1, and Hdc in 1 stitch. End the row with Hdc2tog. (27 stitches)

Row 21: Repeat row 19 (25 stitches)

Row 22: Without chaining 2, turn your work. Start with Hdc2tog, then make Hdc in the next 10 stitches. Continue with Ch 1, skip 1, HdcCS, Ch 1, skip 1, Hdc in 7 stitches, and finish the row with Hdc2tog. (23 stitches)

Row 23: Repeat row 19 (21 stitches)

Row 24: Don't Ch 2, turn. Hdc2tog, Hdc in the next 17 stitches, Hdc2tog (19 stitches)

Row 25: Repeat row 19 (17 stitches)

Row 26: Without chaining 2, turn your work. Begin with Hdc2tog, then make Hdc in the next 6 stitches. Continue with Ch 1, skip 1, HdcCS, Ch 1, skip 1, Hdc in 3 stitches, and finish the row with Hdc2tog. (15 stitches)

Row 27: Chain 2, turn. Make Hdc2tog twice, then Hdc in each stitch across, and finally, make 2 Hdc in the last stitch. (14 stitches)

Row 28: Without chaining 2, turn your work. Start with 2 Hdc in the first stitch, then make Hdc in each stitch across, and end the row with Hdc2tog twice. (13 stitches)

Row 29: Repeat row 27. Then, Ch 12, and connect it to the other end of row 29 with a slip stitch. Finally, Ch 1 and cut the yarn. This will result in a total of 36 stitches, including the 12 stitches from the previous row 29.

Upper Chest

Reattach yarn to one edge of top using a Slst, then work yarn from edge through 12 chains to opposite end.

Row 30: Ch 2, Hdc2tog twice, Hdc in the next 10 stitches, Ch 1, skip 1, HdcCS, Ch 1, skip 1, Hdc in the next 14 stitches, Hdc2tog twice. This will result in 32 stitches.

Row 31: Ch 2, Hdc2tog twice, Hdc in each stitch across, and finish with Hdc2tog twice, for a total of 28 stitches.

Row 32: Ch 2, Hdc2tog twice, Hdc in the next 14 stitches, Ch 1, skip 1, HdcCS, Ch 1, skip 1, Hdc in the next 2 stitches, and Hdc2tog twice more. This will result in 24 stitches.

Row 33: Ch 2, Hdc2tog, Hdc in each stitch across, and finish with Hdc2tog, resulting in 22 stitches.

Row 34: Ch 2, Hdc2tog, Hdc in the next 5 stitches, Ch 1, skip 1, HdcCS, Ch 1, skip 1, Hdc in the next 9 stitches, and Hdc2tog, totaling 20 stitches.

Row 35: Repeat row 33, resulting in 18 stitches. Ch 1 and cut the yarn.

Neckline

Ch 10, reattach yarn to the edge of the project Slst through all 18 stitches from row 35 Ch 12

Row 1: Start with an Hdc in the third chain from the hook and continue with Hdc in the next 6 stitches. Then, Ch 1, skip 1, work an Hdc Cluster Stitch (HdcCS), Ch 1, skip 1, and work Hdc in the next 12 stitches. Repeat the sequence: Ch 1, skip 1, HdcCS, Ch 1, skip 1, and finish the row with Hdc in the last 11 stitches. You should have a total of 38 stitches.

Row 2: Chain 2 and turn. Work an Hdc in each stitch across, maintaining a total of 38 stitches.

Row 3: Chain 2 and turn. Start with an Hdc in the first stitch and continue with Hdc in the next 14 stitches. Then, Ch 1, skip 1, HdcCS, Ch 1, skip 1, and work Hdc in the next 12 stitches. Repeat the sequence: Ch 1, skip 1, HdcCS, Ch 1, skip 1. Finally, finish the row with Hdc in the last 3 stitches, resulting in a total of 38 stitches.

Row 4: Repeat row 2. Ch 1 and cut yarn. (38 stitches)

Heart Finishing

Reattach yarn with a Slst to the 5th of the 12 chain that connects the heart,

Row 1: Begin by chaining 2. Then, work an Hdc into the same stitch where you created the chain and continue with Hdc in the next 3 stitches. You should have a total of 4 stitches.

Row 2: Chain 2 and turn. Perform Hdc2tog twice, resulting in 2 stitches at the end of the row.

Row 3: Turn to Ch. 2. 1 stitch of hdc2tog Work two Sc into the St that joins the heart from row 17 and work Sc around the heart's outline. proceed around the heart and end with a Sc2tog at the beginning. Cut yarn, chain one.

Neck Straps

Ch 50, sc in the second chain from the hook, and slst the yarn to the second row of the neckline. Cut the yarn after slst to starting Ch 1 in each of the 49 stitches across.

Follow the same instructions on the other side.

Back Straps

Ch 120, cut yarn, and secure yarn to one edge of project with Slst.

Repeat the instructions for the other side.

After the back straps are passed between the fourth and seventh rows on both ends in a crisscross manner, weave in all ends.

HAND WARMER

- yarn
- Color A: Ecru; approx 60 yds
- Color B: Charcoal; approx 60 yds
- 5 mm Crochet Hook
- 6 mm Tunisian Crochet Hook
- Yarn Needle
- Scissors

Terms:

BLO Back Loop Only

Ch Chain

Hk Hook

Rem Remaining

Rep Repeat

Sk Skip

Slst Slip Stitch

St(s) Stitch(es)

Tks Tunisian Knit Stitch

Instructions

Band

Row 1: Ch 9(10) using color A and a smaller crochet hook. Sc in every rem ch and in the second ch from hk. Turn and read Ch. 1. 8 and 9 sts

Row 2: Sc in each stitch's BLO, turn, and chain one.

Rep the previous row 26 (or 28) times more. Don't give up easily.

Work should be rotated to equally space 28–30 sc along the band's long edge. Pivot. Don't give up easily.

Hand.

Pick up the working loop with a Tunisian crochet hook on the subsequent row's forward pass. Pull up a loop, insert hk in the next st, and YO. Rep from * to the row's end. (28, 30 HK loops)

*YO and pull through two loops; YO and pull through one loop is the return pass. Rep from * until there's just one loop left on HK.

Rep the previous row forward and then make a return pass until the work is 6.25(7)" from the band edge. Don't give up easily. While embroidering, pull up on the working loop and leave it there.

Make another with B's color.

Finishing

Place the duplicate St in the contrast color for each hand warmer, following the instructions on the following page. The top of the diagram shows the top of the hand warmer.

For every colored square in the diagram, work a duplicate St, beginning at the first skull's lower corner. Work one row higher by moving in the opposite direction after moving from one side of the diagram to the next. The best results will come from this bottom-up, side-to-side approach.

When all four skulls are completed, take up the working loop with the smaller of the two crochet hooks. Fold the hand warmer in half. After inserting hk into the first St on the other side, slip St.

Stitch in the next 8 or 9 stitches to complete the two layers of the hand warmer.

Slip the following seven (8) stitches into the hand warmer, working in only one layer at a time. For the left-hand warmer, choose the layer next to you. For the right-hand warmer, put on the layer furthest from you.

Add the last few hand stitches, making sure the band captures both layers.

Weave in the ends and tie off.

LACE SNOWFLAKE

- hook size 2.5 mm
- Yarn: 185 Yrds (169m)
- weight: Fingering (14 wpi) / Super Fine
- Scissors
- Stitch/place markers

Terms:

- ch – chain
- sl st – slip stitch
- sc – single crochet
- dc – double crochet
- trc – treble crochet
- picot

Instruction

Starting chain: 5 chains, link with a slip St to create a ring.

Row 1: Start with a chain of 6 (where the first 3 chains count as 1 double crochet). Make 1 double crochet in the ring, chain 3, and repeat this sequence 11 times. Finally, slip stitch to join.

Row 2: Repeat the sequence *five times. Slip stitch, chain 1, then make 1 single crochet into the arch. After that, chain 7, make 1 single crochet into the same arch, and then make 2 single crochets into the next arch.

Row 3: Repeat the sequence *five times. Slip stitch, make 1 treble crochet into the same arch, then create 3 double crochets into the same arch. Chain 2, make 2 single crochets into the same arch, 2 treble crochets into the same arch, chain 4 to form a picot, make 1 treble crochet into the same arch, then 3 double crochets into the same arch, 2 chains, and finally, 2 single crochets into the 2 single crochets. Repeat from * into the arch.

Row 4: *Make 2 slip stitches into the 2 single crochets, then make 1 single crochet into the arch. Afterward, make 1 single crochet into the 1 double crochet, chain 3 to create a picot, make 2 single crochets into the 2 double crochets, chain 3 to form another picot, make 1 single crochet into the treble crochet, make 3 single crochets into the picot, chain 4 to create a picot, make 2 single crochets into the picot, make 1 single crochet into the 1 treble crochet, chain 3 to create a picot, make 2 single crochets into the 2 double crochets, chain 3 to form another picot, make 1 single crochet into the double crochet, make 1 single crochet into the arch, make 3 slip stitches into the 3 single crochets, chain 3 to form a picot, then make 1 slip stitch into the single crochet. Repeat from * 5 times, and finally, slip stitch to finish..

MESH TOP

What you need?

- Yarn
- 5mm Hook
- Darning Needle
- Scissors
- St markers
- 2.5cm/1" diameter knitting needle/tube/wooden dowel

Terms:

Ch = Chain

Sl st = Slip Stitch

HDC = Half Double Crochet

FLO = Front Loop

DLO = Dropped Loop Stitch

St(s) = Stitch(es)

Rep = Repeat

Sk = Skip

Measurements cm:

To fit Bust: 76

Panel Width: 43

Length: 52

GAUGE

10cm/4" square = 18.5 stitches wide x 12 rows tall in front loop hdc

Instruction

Body

(make 2)

Starting chain: ch 82

Row 1: Make a half double crochet into the 2nd chain from the hook, and then make a single crochet in each stitch until the end. Turn. (81 stitches)

Row 2: Chain 1, work into the front loops only, make a half double crochet across, and make a half double crochet in the last stitch. Turn. (81 stitches)

Repeat row 2 until row 40.

You can add or remove rows to change the length of your top. Please note that the body is lengthened by 18cm / 7 due to the neck shape and loop detailing.

Neck detail

Row 1: Drop loop: *Push off all loops with your knitting needle if it gets "full. "Draw a loop of ch 1 over the knitting needle, pull it taut, and double-over each stitch till the end. Pull firmly and reattach the last loop to the needle.

Repeat the dlo instructions in each stitch until the end of the row.

Remove the knitting needle, pinch the base of the last dlo, and turn.

<81 loops>

Drop loop row 2: cinch, turn, yarn over, pull up a loop, ch 1, hdc into first double loop, hdc in each double loop to end of row, turn, while hanging on to the double loop.

<81>

Row 3-7: Chain 1, work into the front loops only, make a half double crochet across, and make a half double crochet in the last stitch. Turn. (81 stitches)

Row 8: Work as drop loop row 1. (81 loops)

Row 9: Work as drop loop row 2. (81 stitches)

Row 10: Chain 1, work into the front loops only, make a half double crochet in the first 28 stitches, then slip stitch in the next 25 stitches, work into the front loops only and make a half double crochet across, and make a half double crochet in the last stitch. Turn.

* Make sure your sl sts are not too tight because this can cause the top center to pucker. They should be as comfortable as your HDCs.

<81 loops>

Row 11: Chain 1, work into the front loops only, make a half double crochet in each stitch until the end, and turn. (81 stitches)

Row 12: Chain 1, work into the front loops only, make a half double crochet in the first 26 stitches, then slip stitch in the next 29 stitches, work into the front loops only and make a half double crochet across, and make a half double crochet in the last stitch. Turn. (81 stitches)

Row 13: Work as Row 11. (81 stitches)

Row 14: Chain 1, work into the front loops only, make a half double crochet in the first 24 stitches, then slip stitch in the next 33 stitches, work into the front loops only and make a half double crochet across, and make a half double crochet in the last stitch. Turn. (81 stitches)

Row 15: Work as Row 11. (81 stitches)

Row 16: Chain 1, work into the front loops only, make a half double crochet in the first 22 stitches, then slip stitch in the next 37 stitches, work into the front loops only and make a half double crochet across, and make a half double crochet in the last stitch. Turn. (81 stitches)

Row 17: Work as Row 11. (81 stitches)

Row 18: Chain 1, work into the front loops only, make a half double crochet in the first 26 stitches, then slip stitch in the next 43 stitches, work into the front loops only and make a half double crochet across, and make a half double crochet in the last stitch. Turn. (95 stitches)

Row 19: Work as Row 11. (95 stitches)

Row 20: Chain 1, work into the front loops only, make a half double crochet in the first 32 stitches, then slip stitch in the next 49 stitches, work into the front loops only and make a half double crochet across, and make a half double crochet in the last stitch. Turn. (113 stitches)

Closing

With their right sides inside out, stack the two body panels on top of each other.

Whip stitch around the tops of the shoulders.

To make room for the armholes, reverse the whip St down the sides of the body.

To give you an idea, allow about 18/7 room.

Still, you can resize the armholes to your own length—whatever fits comfortably.

Tie up all of your loose ends.

BOOK 4:
STEP-BY-STEP PROJECTS FOR ADVANCED

SHAWL

Size: 23" long

Yarn

Hook: 7, 4.5 mm

Yarn Needle

Removable St Markers

Gauge: 18 sts x 9 rows = 4" [10 cm] in double crochet

Terms:

ch – chain

dc – double crochet

sc – single crochet

sl st – slip stitch

sp(s) – space(s)

st(s) – stitch(es)

Instruction

Set Up Round

Once you've completed all 86 FDCs, you can slip stitch to the top of the first FDC to form a loop and create a closed foundation row.

Row 1: Place a marker (pm) 2 stitches to the right of the hook. Chain 1, skip 1 stitch, then in the next stitch, work (dc, ch 1, dc, ch 2, pm, dc, ch 1, dc), chain 1, skip 1 stitch, and slip stitch in each of the next 3 stitches. Skip 1 stitch, place a marker, and you should now have 2 double crochets on each side.

Row 2: Chain 1, turn your work. Work a double crochet in the first chain-1 space, then work (dc, ch 1, dc) in the next chain-1 space, remove the marker (rm). In the chain-2 space, work (dc, ch 1, dc, ch 2, place a marker (pm), work a dc, ch 1, dc). In the next chain-1 space, work (dc, ch 1, dc). Work a double crochet in the last chain-1 space, chain 1, slip stitch in the marked stitch, remove the marker (rm), slip stitch in each of the next 2 stitches, skip 1 stitch, and place a marker. You should have 5 double crochets on each side.

Row 3: Chain 1, turn your work. Work (double crochet, chain 1, double crochet) in each of the next 3 chain-1 spaces. Remove the marker (rm). In the chain-2 space, work (double crochet, chain 1, double crochet, chain 2, place a marker (pm), work a double crochet, chain 1, double crochet). In the next 3 chain-1 spaces, work (double crochet, chain 1, double crochet). Chain 1, slip stitch in the marked stitch, remove the marker (rm), slip stitch in each of the next 2 stitches, skip 1 stitch, and place a marker. You should have 8 double crochets on each side.

Row 4: Chain 1, turn your work. Work a double crochet in the first chain-1 space, then work (double crochet, chain 1, double crochet) in the next 4 chain-1 spaces. Remove the marker (rm). In the chain-2 space, work (double crochet, chain 1, double crochet, chain 2, place a marker (pm), work a double crochet, chain 1, double crochet). In the next 4 chain-1 spaces, work (double crochet, chain 1, double crochet). Work a double crochet in the last chain-1 space. Chain 1, slip stitch in the marked stitch, remove the marker (rm), slip stitch in each of the next 2 stitches, skip 1 stitch, and place a marker. You should have 11 double crochets on each side.

Row 5: Chain 2, don't turn your work. Work (double crochet, chain 1, double crochet) in each chain-1 space until you reach the marker. Remove the marker (rm). In the chain-2 space, work (double crochet, chain 1, double crochet, chain 2, place a marker (pm), work a double crochet, chain 1, double crochet). Continue working (double crochet, chain 1, double crochet) in each chain-1 space until you reach the marker. Work a double crochet in the marked stitch, chain 1, place a marker around the chain just made, and work one more double crochet in the same marked stitch. Remove the marker (rm). Skip 2 stitches and work (double crochet, chain 1, double crochet) in the next stitch 20 times. Work a double crochet in the marked stitch, chain 1, place a marker around the chain just made, and work one more double crochet in the same marked stitch. Remove the marker (rm). Slip stitch to the top of the first double crochet made. You should have a total of 72 double crochets.

Row 6: Do not turn your work. Work 4 single crochets in the next chain-1 space, then work 3 single crochets in each chain-1 space until you reach the marker. Remove the marker (rm). In the chain-2 space, work (4 single crochets, chain 2, place a marker (pm), 4 single crochets). Continue working 3 single crochets in each chain-1 space until you reach the marker. Work one more single crochet in the same chain-1 space, then slip stitch in the double crochet just before the marker. Slip stitch in the marked chain-1 space, remove the marker (rm), and place a marker in the next stitch. You should have 26 single crochets on each side.

Row 7: Turn your work. Start with 2 single crochets in the first single crochet, then work a single crochet in each single crochet until you reach the marker. Remove the marker (rm). In the chain-2 space, work (single crochet, chain 2, place a marker (pm), single crochet). Continue working a single crochet in each single crochet until only 1 single crochet remains, then work 2 single crochets in the last single crochet. Slip stitch in the marked chain-1 space, remove the marker (rm), and slip stitch in the next stitch. Place a marker in the next chain-1 space. You should have 28 single crochets on each side.

Row 8: Turn your work. Begin with 2 single crochets in the first single crochet, then work a single crochet in each single crochet until you reach the marker. Remove the marker (rm). In the chain-2 space, work (single crochet, chain 2, place a marker (pm), single crochet). Continue working a single crochet in each single crochet until only 1 single crochet remains, then work 2 single crochets in the last single crochet. Slip stitch in the marked stitch, remove the marker (rm), and slip stitch in the next stitch. Slip stitch in the next chain-1 space, skip 1 double crochet, and place a marker in the next double crochet. You should have 30 single crochets on each side.

Row 9: Chain 1 and turn your work. Begin with (double crochet, chain 1, double crochet) in the first single crochet. Then, skip 2 single crochets and repeat (double crochet, chain 1, double crochet) in the next single crochet. Continue this pattern until you have 2 single crochets left before the point marker. Remove the marker (rm). In the chain-2 space, work (double crochet, chain 1, double crochet, chain 2, place a marker (pm), double crochet, chain 1, double crochet). Now, repeat the pattern of skipping 2 single crochets and working (double crochet, chain 1, double crochet) across the side. After this, chain 1 and slip stitch in the marked chain-1 space, slip stitch in each of the next 2 double crochets, skip the chain-1 space, and place a marker in the next double crochet. You should have 22 double crochets on each side.

Row 10: Chain 1 and turn your work. Start with a double crochet in the first chain-1 space on the side. Then, work (double crochet, chain 1, double crochet) in each chain-1 space until you reach the marker. Remove the marker (rm). In the chain-2 space, work (double crochet, chain 1, double crochet, chain 2, place a marker (pm), double crochet, chain 1, double crochet). Continue by working (double crochet, chain 1, double crochet) in each chain-1 space across the side until only 1 chain-1 space remains on the side. Work a double crochet in the next chain-1 space, chain 1, slip stitch in the marked double crochet, slip stitch in the next chain-1 space, slip stitch in the next double crochet, skip the next double crochet, and place a marker in the next chain-1 space. You should have 25 double crochets on each side.

Row 11: Chain 1, turn your work, and work (double crochet, chain 1, double crochet) in each chain-1 space across the side until you reach the marker. Remove the marker (rm). In the chain-2 space, work (double crochet, chain 1, double crochet, chain 2, place a marker (pm), double crochet, chain 1, double crochet). Continue by working (double crochet, chain 1, double crochet) in each chain-1 space across the side. After that, chain 1, slip stitch in the marked double crochet, remove the marker (rm), slip stitch in the next double crochet, slip stitch in the next chain-1 space, and place a marker in the next chain-1 space. You should now have 28 double crochets on each side.

Row 12: Chain 1, turn your work, and start with a double crochet in the first chain-1 space on the side. Then, work (double crochet, chain 1, double crochet) in each chain-1 space until you reach the marker. Remove the marker (rm). In the chain-2 space, work (double crochet, chain 1, double crochet, chain 2, place a marker (pm), double crochet, chain 1, double crochet). Continue by working (double crochet, chain 1, double crochet) in each chain-1 space across the side until only 1 chain-1 space remains. Work a double crochet in the next chain-1 space, chain 1, slip stitch in the marked chain-1 space, slip stitch in each of the next 2 double crochets, and place a marker in the next chain-1 space. You should now have 31 double crochets on each side.

Row 13: Chain 2, turn your work, and work (double crochet, chain 1, double crochet) in each chain-1 space across the side until you reach the marker. Remove the marker (rm). In the chain-2 space, work (double crochet, chain 1, double crochet, chain 2, place a marker (pm), double crochet, chain 1, double crochet). Continue by working (double crochet, chain 1, double crochet) in each chain-1 space across the side. Work a double crochet in the marked chain-1 space, chain 1, place a marker around the chain just made, and work another double crochet in the marked chain-1 space. Remove the marker (rm). Work (double crochet, chain 1, double crochet) in each chain-1 space until you reach the marker, and work a double crochet in the marked chain-1 space. Chain 1, place a marker around the chain just made, and work another double crochet in the marked stitch. Remove the marker (rm), and finish by slipping stitch to the top of the first double crochet made. You should now have 96 double crochets.

Row 14: Repeat Row 6. You'll have 56 single crochets on each side.

Row 15: Repeat Row 7. You'll have 58 single crochets on each side.

Row 16: Repeat Row 8. You'll have 60 single crochets on each side.

Row 17: Repeat Row 9. You'll have 42 double crochets on each side.

Row 18: Repeat Row 10. You'll have 45 double crochets on each side.

Row 19: Repeat Row 11. You'll have 48 double crochets on each side.

Row 20: Repeat Row 12. You'll have 51 double crochets on each side.

Row 21: Repeat Row 13. You'll have 120 double crochets.

Row 22: Repeat Row 6. You'll have 86 single crochets on each side.

Row 23: Repeat Row 7. You'll have 88 single crochets on each side.

Row 24: Repeat Row 8. You'll have 90 single crochets on each side.

Row 25: Repeat Row 9, but do not place the last marker. You'll have 62 double crochets on each side.

Row 26: Chain 1 and turn. Work a double crochet in the first chain-1 space of the side, then work (double crochet, chain 1, double crochet) in each chain-1 space until you reach the marker. Remove the marker. In the chain-2 space, work (double crochet, chain 1, double crochet, chain 2, place a marker, double crochet, chain 1, double crochet). Then continue to work (double crochet, chain 1, double crochet) in each chain-1 space across the side until only one chain-1 space remains. Work a double crochet in the last chain-1 space, chain 1, and slip stitch in the marked double crochet, and remove the marker. Slip stitch in the next chain-1 space. You should have 65 double crochets on each side.

Continue the rest in rounds from here on.

Row 27: Chain 4 (this counts as the first double crochet and a chain-1, and this applies throughout the pattern), place a marker around the chain you just made, then work another double crochet in the same chain-1 space. Continue to work (double crochet, chain 1, double crochet) in each chain-1 space until you reach the marker. Remove the marker. In the chain-2 space, work (double crochet, chain 1, double crochet, chain 2, place a marker, double crochet, chain 1, double crochet). Then continue by working (double crochet, chain 1, double crochet) in each remaining chain-1 space. Finally, slip stitch to the second chain of the initial chain-3. You should have 140 double crochets in this round.

Row 28: Slip stitch in the marked chain-1 space, remove the marker, chain 4, place a marker around the chain you just made, and then work another double crochet in the same chain-1 space. Continue working (double crochet, chain 1, double crochet) in each chain-1 space until you reach the marker. Remove the marker. In the chain-2 space, work (double crochet, chain 1, double crochet, chain 2, place a marker, double crochet, chain 1, double crochet). Then continue by working (double crochet, chain 1, double crochet) in each remaining chain-1 space. Finally, slip stitch to the second chain of the initial chain-3. You should now have 144 double crochets.

Row 29: Repeat Round 28 to have 148 double crochets.

Row 30: Slip stitch in the marked chain-1 space, remove the marker, chain 1 (this doesn't count as a stitch in this round or throughout the pattern), place a marker, then work 3 single crochets in the same chain-1 space. Continue by working 3 single crochets in each chain-1 space until you reach the marker. Remove the marker. In the chain-2 space, work (single crochet, chain 2, place a marker, single crochet). Then continue by working 3 single crochets in each remaining chain-1 space. Finally, slip stitch to the top of the first single crochet, and place a marker. You should now have 224 single crochets.

Row 31: Chain 3 (this counts as the first double crochet), place a marker in the last chain made, and work a double crochet in each single crochet until you reach the marker. Remove the marker. In the chain-2 space, work (2 double crochets, chain 2, place a marker, 2 double crochets). Then continue by working a double crochet in each remaining single crochet. Finally, slip stitch to the top of the first chain-3 and place a marker. You should have 228 double crochets.

Row 32: Chain 1, place a marker, work a single crochet in each stitch until you reach the marker, remove the marker. In the chain-2 space, work (single crochet, chain 2, place a marker, single crochet). Continue by working a single crochet in each remaining stitch. Finally, slip stitch to the first single crochet and place a marker. You should have 230 single crochets.

Row 33: Start by slip stitching in the next 2 stitches, and then chain 5 (this chain counts as the first double crochet and a chain-2 space throughout the pattern). Work [skip 2 stitches, double crochet in the next stitch, and chain 2] until you reach the marker. Remove the marker. In the chain-2 space, work (double crochet, chain 2, place a marker, double crochet). Chain 2 and double crochet in the next stitch. Continue by working [chain 2, skip 2 stitches, double crochet in the next stitch] until you have 3 stitches left. Chain 2, and slip stitch to the 3rd chain of the initial chain-5. You should have 79 double crochets.

Row 34: Chain 5, then *work a double crochet in the next double crochet, 2 double crochets in the chain-2 space, and [double crochet in the next double crochet, chain 2] three times. Repeat from * until you have 2 double crochets remaining before the marker. Work a double crochet in the next double crochet, 2 double crochets in the chain-2 space, a double crochet in the next double crochet, chain 2, remove the marker, and work (double crochet, chain 2, place a marker, double crochet) in the chain-2 space. Chain 2 and **work a double crochet in the next double crochet, 2 double crochets in the chain-2 space, and [double crochet in the next double crochet, chain 2] three times. Repeat from ** until you have 3 double crochets left, work a double crochet in the next double crochet, 2 double crochets in the chain-2 space, and [double crochet in the next double crochet, chain 2] two times. Finally, slip stitch to the 3rd chain of the initial chain-5. You should have 125 double crochets.

Row 35: Chain 5, work a double crochet in the next double crochet, *chain 2, skip 2 double crochets, double crochet in the next double crochet, and [chain 2, double crochet in the next double crochet] three times. Repeat from * until you have 4 double crochets left before the marker. Chain 2, skip 2 double crochets, [double crochet in the next double crochet, chain 2] two times, remove the marker, and work (double crochet, chain 2, place a marker, double crochet) in the chain-2 space. [Chain 2, double crochet in the next double crochet] two times, **chain 2, skip 2 double crochets, double crochet in the next double crochet, and [chain 2, double crochet in the next double crochet] three times. Repeat from ** until you have 4 double crochets left, chain 2, skip 2 double crochets, and [double crochet in the next double crochet, chain 2] two times. Finally, slip stitch to the 3rd chain of the initial chain-5. You should have 83 double crochets.

Row 36: Begin with a chain-5, then continue with [double crochet in the next double crochet, chain 2] until you reach the marker. Remove the marker. In the chain-2 space, work (double crochet, chain 2, place a marker, double crochet). Keep working [chain 2, double crochet in the next double crochet] until you complete the round. Finish with a chain-2 and slip stitch to the 3rd chain of the initial chain-5. You should have 85 double crochets.

Row 37: Start with a chain-4 (this chain counts as the first double crochet and a chain-1 space). Then, *(double crochet, chain 3, double crochet) in the next double crochet, chain 1, and double crochet in the next double crochet. Repeat this pattern *(double crochet, chain 3, double crochet, chain 1, double crochet in the next double crochet, chain 1) until you reach the marker. Remove the marker. In the chain-2 space, work (double crochet, chain 3, place a marker, double crochet). Continue with **chain 1, double crochet in the next double crochet, chain 1, and (double crochet, chain 3, double crochet) in the next double crochet. Repeat this pattern **(chain 1, double crochet in the next double crochet, chain 1, double crochet in the next double crochet, chain 1) until you complete the round. Finish with a chain-1 and slip stitch to the 3rd chain of the initial chain-4. You should have 129 double crochets.

Row 38: Begin with a chain-1 and a single crochet in the same double crochet. Chain 1. Next, work 5 double crochets in the chain-3 space, chain 1, skip 1 double crochet, single crochet in the next double crochet, chain 1. Repeat this pattern *(5 double crochets in the chain-3 space, chain 1, skip 1 double crochet, single crochet in the next double crochet, chain 1) until you reach the marker. Remove the marker. Place a marker, and then work 7 double crochets in the chain-3 space. Chain 1, and continue with **skip 1 double crochet, single crochet in the next double crochet, chain 1, 5 double crochets in the chain-3 space, chain 1. Repeat this pattern **(skip 1 double crochet, single crochet in the next double crochet, chain 1, 5 double crochets in the chain-3 space, chain 1) until you complete the round. Finally, slip stitch to the top of the beginning single crochet.

Row 39: Begin with a chain-1. Then, *slip stitch in the next double crochet, (chain 3, slip stitch in the next double crochet) 4 times, chain 1, and slip stitch in the single crochet. Chain 1. Continue to repeat this pattern *(slip stitch in the next double crochet, (chain 3, slip stitch in the next double crochet) 4 times, chain 1, slip stitch in the single crochet) until you reach the marker. Remove the marker. Now, slip stitch in the next double crochet, (chain 3, slip stitch in the next double crochet) 3 times, (chain 3, slip stitch in the first chain made) 3 times, slip stitch in the same double crochet, and (chain 3, slip stitch in the next double crochet) 3 times. Next, **chain 1, slip stitch in the single crochet, chain 1, slip stitch in the next double crochet, (chain 3, slip stitch in the next double crochet) 4 times. Repeat this pattern **(chain 1, slip stitch in the single crochet, chain 1, slip stitch in the next double crochet, (chain 3, slip stitch in the next double crochet) 4 times) until you complete the round. Finish with a chain-1 and slip stitch in the first slip stitch of the round.

Finishing: Finish off then weave in ends.

Mosaic Blocks Throw

Size: 54.25" wide x 64.75" (not including border)

Gauge: 12.75 sts and 18 rows = 4" in mosaic St pattern

Materials

Yarn

Hook: I/9 (5.5mm) adjust hook size to maintain gauge

Notions: tapestry needle

Instruction

St Pattern Multiple is 10 +3

With Platinum, chain 174 (10 St multiple, plus 3, plus 1 turning chain)

Set up Row 1: Start by making a single crochet in the second chain from your crochet hook. Then, make a single crochet in each chain across until you reach the end. Afterward, turn your work. You should have a total of 173 single crochets.

Set up Row 2: Begin with a chain of 1. Now, make a single crochet in each of the single crochets from the previous row, working across until you reach the end. Finally, turn your work.

Row 1: Start with a chain of 1 and make a single crochet in the first single crochet. Then, repeat the following pattern: single crochet in the next 3 single crochets, chain 2, skip 1 single crochet twice. After that, make a single crochet in the next 2 single crochets. Repeat this pattern 16 more times, and finish the row with a single crochet in the last 2 single crochets. Finally, turn your work.

Row 2 (Wrong Side - WS): Chain 1, make a single crochet in the first 2 single crochets. Now, repeat the following pattern: single crochet in the next 2 single crochets, [chain 2, single crochet in the next 3 single crochets] twice. Repeat this pattern 16 more times, and end the row with a single crochet in the last 2 single crochets. Change to lace on the last single crochet.

Row 3: Chain 1, make a single crochet in the first single crochet. Then, follow this pattern: single crochet in the next 2 single crochets, chain 2, skip 1 single crochet, special stitch (Sp-dc), single crochet in the next 3 single crochets, Sp-dc, chain 2, skip 1 single crochet, single crochet in the next single crochet. Repeat this pattern 16 more times, and complete the row with a single crochet in the last 2 single crochets. Finally, turn your work.

Row 4: Begin with a chain of 1, then make a single crochet in the first 2 single crochets. Next, follow this pattern: single crochet in the next single crochet, chain 2, single crochet in the next (double crochet, 3 single crochets, double crochet), chain 2, single crochet in the next 2 single crochets. Repeat this pattern 16 more times, and complete the row with a single crochet in the last single crochet. Change to Platinum, and turn your work.

Row 5: Chain 1, make a single crochet in the first single crochet. Then, chain 3 and skip 2 single crochets. Now, follow this pattern: special stitch (Sp-dc), single crochet in the next 5 single crochets, Sp-dc, chain 4, skip 3 single crochets*. Repeat this pattern 16 more times, omitting the final (chain 4, skip 3 single crochets). Finally, chain 3, skip 2 single crochets, and make a single crochet in the last single crochet. Turn your work.

Row 6: Chain 1, make a single crochet in the first single crochet, then chain 3. Now, repeat this pattern: [single crochet in the next (double crochet, 5 single crochets, double crochet), chain 4] 16 times. After the last repeat, make a single crochet in the next (double crochet, 5 single crochets, double crochet), chain 3, and make a single crochet in the last single crochet. Change to Lace, and turn your work.

Row 7: Start with a chain of 1, and make a single crochet in the first single crochet. Then, repeat this pattern: [special stitch (Sp-dc)] twice, chain 2, skip 1 single crochet, single crochet in the next 5 single crochets, chain 2, skip 1 single crochet, Sp-dc. Repeat this pattern 16 more times, and finish the row with a Sp-dc, and a single crochet in the last single crochet. Turn your work.

Row 8: Chain 1, make a single crochet in the first single crochet, then make a single crochet in the next double crochet. Now, follow this pattern: single crochet in the next double crochet, chain 2, single crochet in the next 5 single crochets, chain 2, single crochet in the next 2 double crochets. Repeat this pattern 16 more times, and complete the row with a single crochet in the last single crochet, changing to Platinum. Turn your work.

Row 9: Chain 1, make a single crochet in the first single crochet. Then, repeat this pattern: single crochet in the next 2 single crochets, Sp-dc, chain 2, skip 1 single crochet, single crochet in the next 3 single crochets, chain 2, skip 1 single crochet, Sp-dc, single crochet in the next single crochet. Repeat this pattern 16 more times, and finish the row with a single crochet in the last 2 single crochets. Turn your work.

Row 10: Begin with a chain of 1 and make a single crochet in the first 3 single crochets. Then, follow this pattern: single crochet in the next double crochet, chain 2, single crochet in the next 3 single crochets, chain 2, single crochet in the next (double crochet, 3 single crochets). Repeat this pattern 16 more times, changing to Lace with the last single crochet. Turn your work.

Row 11 (Right Side - RS): Chain 1, make a single crochet in the first single crochet. Then, repeat this pattern: single crochet in the next 3 single crochets, special stitch (Sp-dc), chain 4, skip 3 single crochets, Sp-dc, single crochet in the next 2 single crochets. Repeat this pattern 16 more times, and make a single crochet in the last 2 single crochets. Turn your work.

Row 12: Chain 1, make a single crochet in the first 2 single crochets. Then, follow this pattern: single crochet in the next (2 single crochets, double crochet), chain 4, single crochet in the next (double crochet, 3 single crochets). Repeat this pattern 16 more times, and make a single crochet in the last single crochet, changing to Platinum. Turn your work.

Row 13: Chain 1, make a single crochet in the first single crochet. Then, repeat this pattern: single crochet in the next 3 single crochets, chain 2, skip 1 single crochet, [special stitch (Sp-dc)] 3 times, chain 2, skip 1 single crochet, single crochet in the next 2 single crochets. Repeat this pattern 16 more times, and make a single crochet in the last 2 single crochets. Turn your work.

Row 14: Chain 1, make a single crochet in the first 2 single crochets. Then, follow this pattern: single crochet in the next 2 single crochets, chain 2, single crochet in the next 3 double crochets, chain 2, single crochet in the next 3 single crochets. Repeat this pattern 16 more times, and make a single crochet in the last single crochet, changing to Lace. Turn your work.

Repeat Rows 3 to 14 twenty-two more times, and then repeat Rows 3 to 10 once. Cut the Lace yarn.

Next row (RS): Attach the Lace yarn with a slip stitch in the back loop of only the 4th single crochet. Then, follow this pattern: special stitch (Sp-dc), chain 4, skip 3, Sp-dc, chain 6, skip 5 single crochets. Repeat this pattern 15 more times, then make a Sp-dc, chain 4, skip 3, Sp-dc, and finally, slip stitch in the back loop of the next single crochet. Fasten off, and turn your work.

Next row: Using Platinum yarn, join it with a sc in the first sc of row 10 and in the next 3 sc. *Alt-sc in next dc, sc into the next 3 sc from row 10 ensuring that the chains from row 11 are on the WS of the fabric, alt-sc in next dc, sc into the next 5 sc from row 10 ensuring that the chains from row 11 are on the WS of the fabric; repeat from * 15 times more, alt-sc in next dc, sc into the next 3 sc from row 10 making sure that the chains from row 11 are on the WS of the fabric, alt-sc in next dc, sc into the next 4 sc from row 10, do not change colors, turn.

Finishing Row 1 (RS): Ch 1, sc in each sc to end.

Fasten off.

BORDER

With RS facing, join Platinum to upper right corner of piece.

Round 1: In the corner single crochet, *[single crochet (sc), chain 1, sc], chain 1, skip 1 sc, sc in the next sc, continue this pattern to the last 2 single crochets, chain 1, skip the next sc, [sc, chain 1, sc] in the corner sc. Work [chain 1, sc] 104 times along the side (approximately 3 stitches for every 4 rows), then chain 1. Repeat from * once more, and join with a slip stitch to the beginning sc.

Round 2: Slip stitch in the corner space, *[sc, chain 1, sc] in the corner space, [chain 1, skip sc, sc in the chain-1 space] to the last sc before the corner, chain 1, skip the sc. Repeat from * three more times, and join with a slip stitch to the beginning sc.

Round 3: Repeat Round 2.

Round 4: With the Lace yarn, repeat Round 2.

Rounds 5-7: With the Platinum yarn, repeat Round 2.

Round 8: With the Lace yarn, repeat Round 2.

Rounds 9-11: With the Platinum yarn, repeat Round 2.

Fasten off.

BOOK 5:
STEP-BY-STEP AMIGURUMI PROJECTS

Amigurumi is the art of crocheting small stuffed animals and toys. It's a fun and challenging project that's perfect for beginners.

Are you looking for a new and enchanting craft to dive into? Look no further than the wonderful world of amigurumi! Crafters all around the world have fallen in love with Amigurumi, the art of crocheting tiny plush animals and characters.

The skill of making adorable stuffed animals, monsters, and figures using crochet methods is known as amigurumi, a Japanese name that combines the words "ami" (knitted or crocheted) and "nuigurumi" (stuffed doll). These wonderful sculptures are ideal for gift-giving or as charming decorations since they frequently have enormous heads, petite bodies, and a whimsical touch.

Taking up a new hobby might be intimidating at first since you have to learn a lot of new jargon, make sure you have the necessary supplies, and decide what project to even begin. Here are a few amigurumi crafts to get you going.

BUNNY RABBIT AMIGURUMI

Foundation Row: Ch 26 (36, 47).

Row 1: Sc in second ch from the hook, sc in each remaining ch; turn. [26, 36, 47]

Row 2: Ch 1, sc in each sc to end of row; turn.

Rep Row 2 until rectangle measures approximately 14.5 (19.5, 22)". Fasten off. Weave in ends with a tapestry needle.

Turn your rectangle into a bunny!

When the Rectangle is finished you can use any yarn that is comparable in color to your rectangle and a tapestry needle to perform the next stages. Select a yarn that doesn't break readily if one is available.

A Right Angle Fold

To make one top corner flush with the other rectangular side, fold it down. Mark the location where the top edge meets the rectangle with a St marker, a safety pin, or a strand of thread.

Halve and Place in Markers

Fold top edge toward markers while rectangle is flat once again. Put St marks along the crease's edges.

Fold Vertically in Half

Fold rectangle in half vertically when it has flattened again. Put a marking at the crease on the top edge. There ought to be five St. markers on you now.

Create the Head

Start at the top stitch marker and work your way toward one side marker using a tapestry needle and a doubled-over yarn strand. Proceed to the marker on the opposite side of the rectangle, then return to the top marker. Trim needle, leaving as much of the yarn tail as possible.

Stuff + Scrunch.

Start tightening the stitching around the face, making an effort to equally compress each side of your triangle. While you scrunch, add a handful of fiber fill.

Make Some More Tights.

Simply leave the stitching as it is and go to step 8 after it is as tight as possible. (At now, do not knot.)

Closing the gap.

Pin the rectangle's sides together with St. Markers. Start at the top of the head and work your way down to the bottom of the rectangle using a freshly doubled-over yarn.

Make a basic sewing knot without cutting the yarn. (This keeps the bunny's rear seam from puckering when the bottom is pulled taut.

Stuff + Seam Bottom.

Add as much fiber fill to the body as you choose. Whip St around the bottom of the rectangle with the yarn and needle connected. Pull as tightly as you can, and if the bottom hole is visible, seal it with a few stitches. Tighten up.

Put in a Pom Pom.

Make a pom pom tail and attach it to your rabbit using a piece of cardboard or a pom pom machine.

Include eye dimples.

Bunny cheeks may be held together by using yarn in the chosen eye color. To do this, knot your yarn, put it in the bunny's face, then play around with the knot until it disappears into the face.

Next, create a little St. close to the first eye, then back-stitch the needle through the rabbit head to create a small St. close to the second eye. Pull firmly. Repeat this as often as required to gently indent the eye "sockets."

Complete Face

Sew eyes in place however desired, keeping yarn in place. Use buttons as a substitute. (Of course, avoid giving buttons as gifts to infants or young children as they might choke on them.)

Using a piece of pink yarn, attach a triangular nose. For a unique appearance, consider a "Y" shaped nose.

You already know the saying regarding bunnies, so take some yarn from your stash and crochet a few more!

OCTOPUS SQUISH AMIGURUMI

Terms Used:

FO = fasten off

ch = chain

sl st = slip stitch

sc = single crochet

inc = increase (insert 2 sc in same st)

dec = decrease (sc 2 sts together)

BLO = back loops only

FLO = front loops only

Materials:

Hobbii Baby Snuggle (super bulky "6") yarn in desired color

Black embroidery thread for sewing details

9mm plastic safety eyes (x2)

5mm crochet hook

Stuffing

Yarn needle

Scissors

Instructions

Special Stitch(es):

Tentacle:

- Chain 4.
- Slip stitch in the 2nd chain from the hook.
- Slip stitch in the next stitch.
- Single crochet in the next stitch.

Round 1: Chain 2 and insert 8 single crochets (sc) in the 2nd chain from the hook. (8)

Round 2: Increase (Inc) in each stitch around. (16)

Round 3: *(Single crochet (Sc), Inc) in each of the 8 stitches. (24)

Rounds 4-7: Single crochet (Sc) in each stitch around. (24)

Between R5 and R6, insert plastic safety eyes (9 mm for very bulky yarn and 6 mm for medium weight yarn). Depending on personal preference, place them roughly 4-5 stitches apart. If desired, sew mouth and eyelashes using a yarn needle and black yarn. In the final two rounds, stuff the body as you close the bottom.

Round 8: *(Single crochet (Sc), Decrease (Dec)) in each of the 8 stitches. (16)

Round 9 (tentacle round): For the entire round, work in FLO. Enter the first front loop with an SL. Form a tentacle and slip stitch in front of the next stitch loop.(For each stitch, create a tentacle, then hook into the front loop of the stitch after that. Yo, pass the hook through all three loops.) **To make a total of eight tentacles, repeat around.

Round 10: Work in the unworked back loops from Round 8. Decrease (Dec) around. (8)

Round 11: Decrease (Dec) around. (4) Finish off (FO) with a long tail for sewing the hole shut.

ELEPHANT AMIGURUMI

Terms used:

Rnd: Round

Rw: Row

st: stitch

sc: single crochet

hdc: half double crochet

dc: double crochet

sl st: slip stitch

dec: decrease

inc: increase

Instruction

Ear twice:

Use pink yarn

Row 1: Start with 6 single crochet (sc) stitches in a magic ring. (6)

Row 2: Increase (inc) in each of the 6 stitches. (12)

Row 3: Single crochet (sc) in the next 4 stitches, increase (inc) in the next 3 stitches, and single crochet (sc) in the remaining 5 stitches. (15)

Row 4: Single crochet (sc) in the next 5 stitches, then repeat the pattern (increase in the next stitch, single crochet in the next stitch) three more times, and finally single crochet in the last 4 stitches. (18)

Row 5: Single crochet (sc) in all 18 stitches. (18)

Row 6: Repeat the pattern (single crochet in the next stitch, decrease) six times. (12)

To complete, use an slst.

When you fold the ears to flatten them, make sure the increases are at the bottom of the ears. Furthermore, make sure the tip of the ear is where the last round ends.

Body:

Use pink yarn

Rows 2-3: Single crochet (sc) in all 6 stitches. (6)

Row 4: Repeat the pattern (single crochet, increase in the next stitch) three times. (9)

Row 5: Single crochet (sc) in all 9 stitches. (9)

Row 6: Repeat the pattern (single crochet in the next 2 stitches, increase in the next stitch) three times. (12)

Mark the 7th and 14th stitches of round 7 with stitch markers. You will use these markers to help you place the safety eyes later.

Row 7: Single crochet in the next 3 stitches, then increase 6 times, and finally single crochet in the next 3 stitches. (18)

Row 8: Single crochet in the next 3 stitches, then repeat the sequence (single crochet, increase in the next stitch) 6 times, and finally single crochet in the next 3 stitches. (24)

Row 9: Repeat this sequence 3 times: Single crochet in the next 7 stitches, increase in the next stitch. (27)

Row 10: Single crochet in all 27 stitches. (27)

Row 11: Single crochet in the next 5 stitches. For the next 6 stitches, insert your hook through the flattened ear stitches and the body, then single crochet. Single crochet in the next 7 stitches, and for the next 6 stitches, insert your hook through the other flattened ear stitches and the body, then single crochet. single crochet in the last 3 stitches. (27)

Between rounds 7 and 8, insert the safety eyes into the previously designated stitches.

Rows 12-18: Single crochet in all 27 stitches. (27)

Row 19: *(Single crochet in the next 7 stitches, decrease) repeat 3 times. (24)

Row 20: *(Single crochet in the next 2 stitches, decrease) repeat 6 times. (18)

Row 21: *(Single crochet in the next stitch, decrease) repeat 6 times. (12)

Stuff the body with filling.

Row 22: Decrease 6 times. (6)

Sew the head through the front loops of each crochet St made in the previous round, using the remaining strand of yarn. Pull the yarn tightly to close the hole. Now use a needle to thread the end of the yarn through the hole. It's important not to cut the yarn between rounds 21 and 22, but to sew it so that it protrudes beyond the body. This end of yarn will be used to crochet the tail later on.

To continue, make a little loop by inserting your crochet hook into the body directly below round 21. Then, using a gentle grip, thread the yarn through the body to create a loop.

The tail can be created in two distinct ways: by crocheting in the loops on the back of the tail or the side loops. The first way yields a finer-tuned tail, although it is a little more difficult.

Choice 1: Chapter 5. Proceed to work into the loop on the opposite side of the chain.

Slip St in the next three stitches, work in the second chain from the hook, and slip St in the body.

Stuff the remaining yarn into the body lastly.

Choice 2: Chain 4. Crochet into side loop of chain.

Slip St in the next three stitches, work in the second chain from the hook, and slip St in the body.

Stuff the remaining yarn into the body lastly.

Cut two 4 in./11 cm pink yarn strands.

The two strands you have should be folded. Then secure them to the tip of the tail. Cut the yarn to the right length before using it.

Legs four times:

Use pink yarn

Row 1: Start with 6 single crochets in a magic ring.

Row 2: Single crochet in all 6 stitches.

Finish with a slip stitch.

Position the legs on the bottom of the body, leaving 4 rows and 4 stitches separating the front and back legs, respectively.

Mini heart: Use red yarn.

Row 1: Single crochet, 3 double crochets, 2 single crochets, 1 half double crochet, 2 single crochets, and 3 double crochets in a magic ring.

Use a slip St to finish off in the first sc of round 1.

St the leftover yarn through the center of the heart's front side. A lengthy length of yarn should be left over to sew the body's heart. Sew the heart onto the body's side.

The heart is tiny; use your fingers to form it slightly.

KOALA AMIGURUMI

- Size: 24 cm / 10 inch
- Scissors
- Tapestry needles
- hook 2.5 mm 4/0

Instruction

Body:

Row 1: Start with 6 single crochets in a magic ring [6].

Row 2: Increase in each of the 6 stitches [12].

Row 3: (Single crochet, increase in the next stitch) repeated 6 times [18].

Row 4: (Single crochet in the next 2 stitches, increase in the next stitch) repeated 6 times [24].

Row 5: (Single crochet in the next 3 stitches, increase in the next stitch) repeated 6 times [30].

Row 6: (Single crochet in the next 4 stitches, increase in the next stitch) repeated 6 times [36].

Row 7: Single crochet in all 36 stitches [36].

Row 8: (Single crochet in the next 5 stitches, increase in the next stitch) repeated 6 times [42].

Rows 9-10: Single crochet in all 42 stitches [42].

Row 11: (Single crochet in the next 6 stitches, increase in the next stitch) repeated 6 times [48].

Rows 12-18: Single crochet in all 48 stitches [48].

Insert 8 mm safety eyes between round 10-11 with an interspace of 9 stitches.

Row 19: (Single crochet in the next 6 stitches, decrease) repeated 6 times [42].

Row 20: (Single crochet in the next 5 stitches, decrease) repeated 6 times [36].

Row 21: (Single crochet in the next 4 stitches, decrease) repeated 6 times [30].

Row 22: (Single crochet in the next 3 stitches, decrease) repeated 6 times [24].

Stuff the body with toy filling.

Row 23: (Single crochet in the next 2 stitches, decrease) repeated 6 times [18].

Row 24: (Single crochet in the next stitch, decrease) repeated 6 times [12].

Row 25: Decrease 6 times [6].

Sew shut, leaving a long tail of yarn. Pull the yarn tail taut to complete each remaining St by weaving it through the front loop with your yarn needle. Incorporate the yarn's end.

Ear 2x:

Row 1: Start with 6 single crochets in a magic ring [6].

Row 2: Increase 6 times [12].

Rows 3-5: Single crochet in all 12 stitches [12].

Use a slip stitch to finish.

To flatten the ears, fold them.

The Inside Ear twice:

Row 1: Begin with 6 single crochets in a magic ring [6].

Use a slip stitch to finish.

Sew the ear's interior to its exterior.

Sew the ears onto rounds 6 through 10.

Nose:

Row 1: Start with 6 single crochets in a magic ring [6].

Row 2: (Single crochet in the next stitch, increase) repeat 3 times [9].

Use a slip stitch to finish.

Sew the snout onto rounds 9 through 11.

Leg twice:

Row 1: Start with 6 single crochets in a magic ring [6].

Row 2: Increase in each stitch around, repeating 6 times [12].

Rows 3-5: Single crochet in all 12 stitches [12].

Finish with a slip stitch.

Stitch legs onto rounds 16–20, spaced 10 stitches apart between stitches. Stuff the legs with toy stuffing when you are almost finished stitching them to the body.

Arm twice:

Row 1: Start with 5 single crochets in a magic circle [5].

Row 2: Increase in each stitch around, repeating 5 times [10].

Rows 3-4: Single crochet in all 10 stitches [10].

Use a slip stitch to secure.

Stitch the arms onto rounds 15–17. Stuff the arms with toy stuffing when you are almost finished sewing the legs onto the body.

Belly:

Row 1: Begin with 8 single crochets in a magic ring [8].

Row 2: Increase in each of the 8 stitches [16].

Row 3: Repeat (single crochet in the next stitch, increase) 8 times [24].

Row 4: Single crochet in all 24 stitches [24].

Finish with a slip stitch.

St the abdomen to rounds 15–21.

Your koala is finished now!

FOX AMIGURUMI

What you need

These are the supplies I made use of. You can use different materials in their place. Simply use a thicker or thinner yarn or crochet hook to create an amigurumi that is larger or smaller.

- Orange cotton: 281
- Black cotton: 110
- White cotton: 105
- Synthetic Poly filling
- 1 safety eyes size: 8 mm

Using a 5.0 mm hook and extremely bulky orange, black, and white yarn, the fox's eyes measure 16 mm.

Body:

Round 1: Begin with 6 single crochets in a magic ring [6].

Round 2: Increase in each of the 6 stitches [12].

Round 3: Repeat (single crochet, increase in the next stitch) 6 times [18].

Round 4: Repeat (single crochet in the next 2 stitches, increase in the next stitch) 6 times [24].

Round 5: Repeat (single crochet in the next 3 stitches, increase in the next stitch) 6 times [30].

Round 6: Repeat (single crochet in the next 4 stitches, increase in the next stitch) 6 times [36].

Rounds 7-8: sc in all 36 st [36]

Round 9: Repeat (single crochet in the next 5 stitches, increase in the next stitch) 6 times [42].

Round 10: Single crochet in all 42 stitches [42].

Round 11: Repeat (single crochet in the next 6 stitches, increase in the next stitch) 6 times [48].

Rounds 12-15: Single crochet in all 48 stitches [48].

Insert 8 mm safety eyes between round 12 and round 13 with a gap of 12 stitches between them.

Round 16: Repeat (single crochet in the next 6 stitches, decrease) 6 times [42].

Round 17: Repeat (single crochet in the next 5 stitches, decrease) 6 times [36].

Round 18: Repeat (single crochet in the next 4 stitches, decrease) 6 times [30].

Round 19: Repeat (single crochet in the next 3 stitches, decrease) 6 times [24].

Stuff the body with toy fiberfilling and continue stuffing as you go.

Round 20: Repeat (single crochet in the next 2 stitches, decrease) 6 times [18].

Round 21: Repeat (single crochet in the next stitch, decrease) 6 times [12].

Round 22: Decrease 6 times [6].

Sew shut, leaving a long tail of yarn. Pull the yarn tail taut to complete each remaining St by weaving it through the front loop with your yarn needle. Incorporate the yarn's end.

Snout:

Round 1: Begin with a magic ring and make 6 single crochets in it. You'll have 6 stitches.

Round 2: Increase in each of the 6 stitches, so you'll have 12 stitches in total.

Round 3: Just single crochet in each of the 12 stitches. No increases. You'll still have 12 stitches.

Round 4: In this round, single crochet in the first stitch, then increase in the next one. Repeat this pattern 6 times, and you'll have 18 stitches at the end.

Round 5: Single crochet in the first two stitches, then increase in the next one. Repeat this pattern 6 times, and you'll have 24 stitches in total.

Round 6: Simply single crochet in all 24 stitches.

With a slst, fasten off, leaving a long tail for stitching.

Just before stitching the beak onto the body, stuff the snout with toy fiberfill.

In the space between rounds 9 and 18, sew the snout to the head.

Nose:

Round 1: Begin by making 5 single crochets in a magic circle.

With a slst, fasten off, leaving a long tail for stitching.

St the nose to the first round of the snout.

Ear twice:

Round 1: Create a magic circle and crochet 4 single crochets into it. You'll have a total of 4 stitches in this round.

Round 2: Increase by making 2 single crochets in each of the 4 stitches. This will give you a total of 8 stitches in this round.

Round 3: In this round, crochet 1 single crochet in the next stitch, then make an increase by crocheting 2 single crochets in the next stitch. Repeat this pattern 4 times, and you'll have a total of 12 stitches in this round.

Round 4: Crochet 2 single crochets in the next stitch, then in the following stitches, crochet 2 single crochets, and repeat this pattern 4 times. You'll have a total of 16 stitches in this round.

Round 5: Crochet 3 single crochets in the next stitch, then in the following stitches, crochet 3 single crochets, and repeat this pattern 4 times. You'll have a total of 20 stitches in this round.

Rounds 6-7: Simply crochet 1 single crochet in each of the 20 stitches in these rounds.

With a slst, fasten off, leaving a long tail for stitching.

To flatten the ears, fold them.

Inside ear twice: ch 6

Row 1: Begin in the second chain from the hook and crochet a single crochet in the next 5 stitches. Chain 1, and then turn your work. You will have 5 stitches.

Row 2: Skip the first stitch, and single crochet in the next 4 stitches. Chain 1, and turn your work. You will have 4 stitches.

Row 3: Skip the first stitch, and single crochet in the next 3 stitches. Chain 1, and turn your work. You will have 3 stitches.

Row 4: Skip the first stitch, and single crochet in the next 2 stitches. Chain 1, and turn your work. You will have 2 stitches.

Row 5: Skip the first stitch, then begin in the second chain from your hook, and single crochet in the next stitch. You will have 1 stitch.

Leave a long tail for stitching and fasten off.

Sew the inner ear into the outside ear.

Sew the ears to the body in the intervals of rounds 5–13.

Feet twice:

Round 1: Begin by making 6 single crochets (sc) in a magic circle. This creates 6 stitches in the round.

Round 2: Increase in each of the 6 stitches, resulting in a total of 12 stitches in the round.

Rounds 3-4: Single crochet in each of the 12 stitches, maintaining the same number of stitches in the round.

Round 5: Single crochet in the next 2 stitches, then decrease (dec) by crocheting 2 stitches together. Repeat this pattern 3 times, and you'll end up with 9 stitches in the round.

With a slst, fasten off, leaving a long tail for stitching.

The feet should be folded to flatten them and then sewn to the body's bottom.

Tail:

Round 1: Create a magic circle and single crochet (sc) 4 times into it. This forms 4 stitches in the round.

Round 2: Increase (inc) in each of the 4 stitches, resulting in a total of 8 stitches in the round.

Rounds 3-4: Single crochet in all 8 stitches, maintaining the same stitch count in the round.

Round 5: Single crochet in the next stitch, then increase (inc) in the next stitch. Repeat this pattern 4 times, giving you a total of 12 stitches in the round.

Round 6: Perform a single crochet in all 12 stitches, keeping the same number of stitches in the round.

Round 7: Single crochet in the next 3 stitches, then increase (inc) in the next stitch. Repeat this pattern 4 times, resulting in 20 stitches in the round.

Rounds 8-9: Single crochet in all 20 stitches, maintaining the stitch count in the round.

Change yarn

Round 10: Single crochet in the next 3 stitches, then decrease (dec) in the next stitch. Repeat this pattern 6 times, resulting in 16 stitches in the round.

Rounds 11-12: Single crochet in all 16 stitches, keeping the same number of stitches in the round.

Round 13: Single crochet in the next 2 stitches, then decrease (dec) in the next stitch. Repeat this pattern 6 times, giving you 12 stitches in the round.

Round 14: Single crochet in all 12 stitches, maintaining the stitch count in the round.

Round 15: Single crochet in the next stitch, then decrease (dec) in the next stitch. Repeat this pattern 6 times, resulting in 8 stitches in the round.

Rounds 16-18: Perform a single crochet in all 8 stitches, keeping the same number of stitches in the round.

With a slst, fasten off, leaving a long tail for stitching.

Stuff the tail with food. Back of the tail should be sewn in between rounds 14 and 18.

Your fox is finished now!

DOG AMIGURUMI

Crochet a very cute Pug dog Amigurumi.

What you need?

6 cm / 2 inch:

- Beige color:
- Brown color
- Black color

Synthetic Poly filling

yarn: When you crochet the dog, its body may appear a little too oval, but that won't matter because stuffing will make it look perfect.

- Scissors
- Tapestry needles with blunt point, nr. 16 or 17
- Pins
- hook size 2.5 mm 4/0 for the cotton

Terms:

Rw: Row

Rnd: Round

st: stitch

sc: single crochet

sl st: slip stitch

dec: decrease

inc: increase

instruction

Body:

Round 1: Begin by making 6 single crochets (sc) in a magic ring. You'll have 6 stitches in this round.

Round 2: Increase (inc) in each of the 6 stitches, so you end up with 12 stitches in this round.

If you haven't already, place a piece of yarn to mark the start of round 3. This will help you count the stitches later.

Round 3: In this round, do 1 single crochet (sc), then increase (inc) in the next stitch. Repeat this pattern 6 times, resulting in 18 stitches in the round.

Round 4: Single crochet (sc) in the next 2 stitches, then increase (inc) in the following stitch. Repeat this pattern 6 times, so you'll have 24 stitches in the round.

Round 5: Single crochet (sc) in the next 7 stitches, and then increase (inc) in the next stitch. Repeat this pattern 3 times, giving you a total of 27 stitches.

Rounds 6 to 13: Single crochet (sc) in all 27 stitches in each of these rounds, keeping the same number of stitches in each round.

If desired, two strands of folded yarn can be secured on the inside of the dog's body and sewn at the top between rows 9 and 10. This will enable the dog to be turned into a keychain.

Place stitches between stitches 5 and 14 and between rows 3 and 4 on the body.

Round 14: In this round, single crochet (sc) in the next 7 stitches, and then decrease (dec) in the next stitch. Repeat this pattern 3 times, resulting in 24 stitches in the round.

Round 15: Single crochet (sc) in the next 2 stitches, and then decrease (dec) in the next stitch. Repeat this pattern 6 times, so you'll have 18 stitches in the round. At this point, fill the head with the stuffing material.

Round 16: In this round, single crochet (sc) in the next stitch, and then decrease (dec) in the next stitch. Repeat this pattern 6 times, giving you 12 stitches in the round.

Round 17: For the final round, decrease (dec) in each of the 6 stitches, leaving you with 6 stitches.

Sew the head through the front loops of each crochet St made in the previous round, using the remaining strand of yarn. Pull the yarn tightly to close the hole. Now use a needle to thread the end of the yarn through the hole.

Ears twice:

Round 1: Begin with 4 single crochet (sc) stitches in a magic ring, resulting in a total of 4 stitches in the round.

Round 2: In this round, single crochet (sc) in the first stitch, and then increase (inc) in the next stitch. Repeat this pattern 2 times, and you'll have 6 stitches in the round.

Rounds 3-4: Continue by single crocheting (sc) in all 6 stitches in each of these two rounds, maintaining a total of 6 stitches in each round.

Leave a long tail for stitching and fasten off. Bring the ears flat.

Sew ear round 4 onto body round 7, leaving 6 stitches between each ear.

Sew the tips of the ears to the body after folding them.

Snout:

Round 1: Begin by making 6 single crochet (sc) stitches in a magic ring, creating a total of 6 stitches in the round.

Round 2: In this round, start with a single crochet (sc) in the first stitch, and then increase (inc) in the next stitch. Repeat this pattern 3 times, resulting in a total of 9 stitches in the round.

Round 3: Continue by single crocheting (sc) in the next 2 stitches, followed by an increase (inc) in the next stitch. Repeat this pattern 3 times, and you'll have 12 stitches in the round.

Leave a long tail for stitching and fasten off.

Between rounds one and two, use black yarn to embroider a nose on the snout.

Sew the muzzle to the body, with the muzzle's top falling below round 2 and its bottom above round 5.

Legs four times:

In Round 1, you'll create your work as follows: Start with a magic ring and crochet 6 single crochet (sc) stitches into it. This round will have a total of 6 stitches when you're done.

Leave a long tail for stitching and fasten off.

Put the legs on the underside of the body, with 4 rows between the front and rear legs and 4 stitches between the front and rear legs.

Tail: Ch 9

For Row 1, begin in the second chain from your hook, then slip stitch in each of the next 8 stitches. When you're finished, you should have a total of 8 slip stitches in this row.

Leave a long length of yarn for stitching once you fasten off.

Curl the tail by twisting it with your fingers.

Sew the tail between rounds 15 and 16 on top of the body.

Your puppy is finished now!

CAT AMIGURUMI

Discover how to make this cute cat Amigurumi.

When you crochet the cat, its body may appear a little too oval, but that won't matter because stuffing will make it look normal.

What you need?

- Scissors
- Tapestry needles
- Pins
- hook size 2.5 mm 4/0 for the cotton

Instruction

Body:

Round 1: make a magic ring and crochet 6 single crochets (sc) into it. You'll have a total of 6 stitches in this round.

Round 2: increase (inc) in each of the 6 stitches from the previous round. This means you crochet 2 single crochets into each of those 6 stitches. You'll end up with 12 stitches in this round.

Round 3: crochet 1 single crochet, then increase (inc) in the next stitch. Repeat this pattern 6 times, and you'll have a total of 18 stitches in this round.

Round 4: single crochet (sc) in the next 2 stitches, then increase (inc) in the following stitch. Repeat this sequence 6 times, and you'll have 24 stitches in this round.

If you'd like, you can sew two strands of folded yarn into the top of the cat and secure them inside the head to make it into a keychain.

Round 5: simply single crochet (sc) in each of the 24 stitches from the previous round. There are no increases or decreases in this round.

Round 6: start by single crocheting in the next 3 stitches, and then increase (inc) in the following stitch. Repeat this pattern 6 times, and you'll have a total of 30 stitches in this round.

Round 7: single crochet (sc) in all 30 stitches from the previous round. No increases or decreases in this round either.

If you haven't previously, use a piece of yarn to indicate the start of round 8 so you can count the stitches later.

Round 8: begin by single crocheting (sc) in the next 9 stitches, and then increase (inc) in the following stitch. Repeat this pattern 3 times, and you'll have a total of 33 stitches in this round.

Rounds 9 and 10: just single crochet (sc) in all 33 stitches from the previous round.

Round 11: start by single crocheting in the next 9 stitches, and then decrease (dec) in the following stitch. Repeat this pattern 3 times, and you'll have 30 stitches in this round.

St one eye between stitches 13 and 14, and the other between stitches 18 and 19, over round 8. St the nose, which is one St wide, in between rounds eight and nine. Between the nose and the eyes are two stitches.

St the top and bottom stripes on the body between rounds 8 and 9, and between rounds 9 and 10. The stripes on the front and back top (between rounds 8 and 9) and the front and back bottom (between rounds 9 and 10) are each two stitches wide and three stitches wide, respectively.

Sew three stripes in the front and three in the back, using four rounds for the front and three rounds for the back of the head.

Round 13: single crochet (sc) in the next 2 stitches and then decrease (dec) in the following stitch. Repeat this pattern 6 times, and you'll have 18 stitches in this round.

Round 14: simply single crochet (sc) in all 18 stitches from the previous round.

Round 15: begin by single crocheting in the next 2 stitches, and then increase (inc) in the following stitch. Repeat this pattern 6 times, and you'll have 24 stitches in this round.

Rounds 16-18 are straightforward - just single crochet (sc) in all 24 stitches in each of these rounds.

St the stripes onto the cat's back: the upper stripe should be sewn between rounds 15 and 16, and the lower stripe between rounds 16 and 17. There are four stitches in the bottom stripe and six stitches in the top stripe.

Round 19: begin by single crocheting (sc) in the next stitch, then decrease (dec) in the following stitch. Repeat this pattern 8 times, and you'll have 16 stitches left in this round.

Round 20: simply decrease (dec) 8 times, which will reduce your stitch count to 8.

After that, you can stuff the body with toy fiberfilling.

Finally, for **Round 21**, decrease (dec) 4 times, and you'll be left with just 4 stitches. This will finish off your project.

Leave a long tail for stitching and fasten off.

Using the last strand of yarn, complete the head by sewing it through the front loops of each crochet St created in the previous round. To seal the hole, pull the yarn tightly. Now thread the yarn end through the hole using a needle.

Ear twice:

Round 1: Begin by single crocheting (sc) 4 times in a magic circle, creating 4 stitches in total.

Round 2: Repeat the sequence of single crochet (sc) followed by an increase (inc) 2 times in total. This will result in 6 stitches at the end of the round.

Round 3: Crochet 2 single crochets (sc) followed by an increase (inc) in the next stitch, and repeat this sequence twice. You'll end up with 8 stitches in this round.

Round 4: Perform 3 single crochets (sc) followed by an increase (inc) in the next stitch, and repeat this sequence twice to get a total of 10 stitches at the end of this round.

With a slst, fasten off, leaving a long tail for stitching.

Sew the ear between rounds 3 and 8 after folding it to make it more flat.

Tail: Use grey yarn

Round 1: Begin by making 6 single crochets (sc) in a magic circle, creating a total of 6 stitches.

Round 2: Repeat the sequence of 1 single crochet (sc) followed by an increase (inc) in the next stitch, and do this 3 times. This will give you a total of 9 stitches in this round.

Rounds 3-4: Crochet 1 single crochet (sc) in each of the 9 stitches in both of these rounds.

Round 5: Alternate between 1 single crochet (sc) in the next stitch and a decrease (dec) 3 times. You'll end up with 6 stitches at the end of this round.

Rounds 6-11: Continue with 1 single crochet (sc) in each of the 6 stitches for these rounds.

Leave a long tail for stitching and fasten off.

Fill the tail with fiberfill for a toy.

Using the remaining strand of yarn, finish the tail by threading it through the front loops of each crochet St created in the previous round. To seal the hole, pull the yarn tightly. Now thread the yarn end through the hole using a needle.

Sew the tail onto the body's 18th round. The beginning of the tail is positioned somewhat below round 19.

Feet twice:

Round 1: you'll create 6 single crochets (sc) by starting in a magic circle.

With a slst, fasten off, leaving a long tail for stitching.

In between rounds 17 and 20, sew the feet in front of the torso.

Your pet is finished now!

Bat Amigurumi

What you need?

– Scissors

– Tapestry needles with blunt point, nr. 16 or 17

– Pins

–hook size 2.5 mm 4/0 for the cotton

Instruction

Body:

Round 1: create a circle with 6 single crochet stitches (sc) in it, resulting in 6 stitches in total.

Round 2: increase (inc) in each of the 6 stitches from the previous round. This will double the stitch count to 12 in Round 2.

Round 3: alternate between a single crochet (sc) and an increase (inc) in each of the 6 stitches from the previous round. This brings the total stitch count to 18 in Round 3.

Round 4 involves making one single crochet in the first stitch, then another single crochet in the next stitch, followed by an increase (inc) in the next stitch. Repeat this pattern 6 times, and you'll end up with 24 stitches in Round 4.

Round 5: simply make one single crochet in each of the 24 stitches from the previous round.

Round 6: repeat a pattern: make one single crochet in the first three stitches, then increase (inc) in the next stitch. Do this pattern 6 times to have 30 stitches in Round 6.

Rounds 7 and 8 are straightforward: just make one single crochet in each of the 30 stitches in these rounds.

Round 9: follow this pattern: make one single crochet (sc) in the first 4 stitches, then increase (inc) in the next stitch. Repeat this pattern 6 times to have a total of 36 stitches in Round 9.

Rounds 10 - 12: simply make one single crochet in each of the 36 stitches in these rounds.

Round 13 involves making one single crochet in each of the first 4 stitches, followed by a decrease (dec) in the next stitch. Repeat this pattern 6 times, resulting in a total of 30 stitches in Round 13.

Sew the eyes using 6 stitches between each, covering rounds 10 and 11. Sew the nose, which is two stitches wide, in between rounds 11 and 12. Between the nose and the eyes are two sutures.

Round 14: you'll make one single crochet (sc) in each of the first 3 stitches, followed by a decrease (dec) in the next stitch. Repeat this pattern 6 times to have a total of 24 stitches in Round 14.

Round 15: make one single crochet in each of the first 2 stitches, followed by a decrease (dec) in the next stitch. Repeat this pattern 6 times to have a total of 18 stitches in Round 15.

Round 16: simply make one single crochet in each of the 18 stitches.

Round 17 involves making one single crochet in each of the first 2 stitches, followed by an increase (inc) in the next stitch. Repeat this pattern 6 times, resulting in a total of 24 stitches in Round 17.

Rounds 18 – 21: make one single crochet in each of the 24 stitches in these rounds.

Round 22: make one single crochet in the first stitch, followed by a decrease (dec) in the next stitch. Repeat this pattern 8 times to have a total of 16 stitches in Round 22.

Sew the feet over round 20 and 21, there are 2 stitches between both feet.

Round 23: you'll decrease (dec) in each of the 8 stitches, resulting in a total of 8 stitches in this round.

After that, stuff the body with toy fiberfilling to make it plump and three-dimensional.

Round 24: you'll make one single crochet (sc) in each of the first 2 stitches, followed by a decrease (dec) in the next stitch. Repeat this pattern 2 times, and you'll have a total of 6 stitches in Round 24.

Leave a long tail for stitching and fasten off.

Sew the last strand of yarn through the front loops of each crochet St formed in the previous round to complete the body. To seal the hole, pull the yarn tightly. Now thread the yarn end through the hole using a needle.

Ear twice:

Round 1: make 4 single crochet stitches (sc) in a magic ring.

Round 2: do one single crochet (sc) followed by an increase (inc) in the next stitch, and repeat this pattern once more, so you have 6 stitches in total.

Round 3: make one single crochet (sc) in each of the next 2 stitches, followed by an increase (inc) in the next stitch, and repeat this pattern once more, resulting in 8 stitches.

Round 4: create one single crochet (sc) in each of the next 3 stitches, followed by an increase (inc) in the next stitch, and repeat this pattern once more, ending with 10 stitches in total.

Round 5: make a single crochet (sc) in all 10 stitches to complete this round.

With a slst, fasten off, leaving a long tail for stitching.

Sew the flattened ear between rounds two and six. Fold the ear.

Wing twice:

Round 1: Start with 4 single crochet stitches (sc) in a magic circle.

Round 2: Increase (inc) in each of the 4 stitches, resulting in 8 stitches.

Round 3: Make a single crochet (sc) in all 8 stitches.

Round 4: In each of the 4 stitches, make 1 single crochet (sc) followed by an increase (inc), giving you a total of 12 stitches.

Round 5: Repeat the pattern of 1 single crochet (sc) followed by an increase (inc) six times, resulting in 18 stitches.

Round 6: In the first stitch, make a single crochet (sc). Then, repeat the pattern of 2 single crochets (sc) followed by an increase (inc) in the next stitch. Do this a total of 6 times, and you'll have 24 stitches.

Round 7: Create a single crochet (sc) in the next stitch, then follow the pattern: single crochet (sc), half double crochet (hdc), hdc + double crochet (dc) + hdc, hdc, in the next stitch. Repeat this pattern five more times. In the next stitch, make a single crochet (sc), and then create an hdc + dc + hdc, resulting in a total of 36 stitches.

Round 8: Make a single crochet (sc) in the next stitch, then a slip stitch (slst) in the following stitch. Don't crochet in any of the remaining stitches.

Leave a long tail for stitching and fasten off.

On rounds 18 and 19, sew the wings onto the rear of the body.

Your bat is finished now!

CACTUS IN A POT KEYCHAIN

crochet a very cute cactus keychain in a pot with flower.

What you need

- Scissors
- Tapestry needles
- Pins

Instruction

Cactus: Ch 12

Row 1: Begin in the second chain from the hook, and make a single crochet (sc) in each of the next 11 stitches. After that, chain 1 and turn your work. (11 stitches in total)

Rows 2 to 10: Work in the back loop only (BLO), making single crochets in the next 11 stitches for each row. After each row, chain 1 and turn your work. (11 stitches in each row)

Crochet row 10 and the other side of the chain together.

Leave a long tail for stitching and fasten off.

Using your yarn needle, seal the top of the cactus now by weaving the yarn tail through the top loops of each subsequent row. Sew via loops 1, 3, 5, and so on. These are the rows that the cactus has in between the rows that give it its bumps. To shut, pull it tightly. Make a little knot to secure the yarn on the opposite side of the cactus after weaving the yarn through to the other hole. Insist on cramming the cactus.

Pot:

Round 1: Begin by making 8 single crochets (sc) in a magic circle. (8 stitches)

Round 2: Increase in each of the 8 stitches, resulting in 16 stitches in this round.

Round 3: Work in the back loop only (BLO) and make a single crochet in each of the 16 stitches.

Round 4: Make a single crochet in all 16 stitches.

Round 5: In this round, you'll make a pattern: single crochet in the next 3 stitches, then increase in the next stitch. Repeat this pattern 4 times, and you'll end up with 20 stitches.

Round 6: Make a single crochet in all 20 stitches.

Round 7: This round is worked in the front loop only (FLO), and you'll make a single crochet in all 20 stitches using the front loops.

Fasten off, sew in the yarn end, don't sew over the FLO of Rnd 7.

Soil:

Round 8: Attach brown yarn to the back loop only (BLO) of the first stitch from round 7 of the cactus. Then, make a single crochet in all 20 stitches. This round helps create the top of the pot.

Round 9: Work a decrease in each of the 20 stitches a total of 10 times. This will decrease the stitch count to 10, and you'll see the pot shape forming.

Before continuing, stuff the pot part of your amigurumi with filling.

Round 10: Make a decrease in each of the 10 stitches a total of 5 times. This round will further close the top of the pot, leaving you with only 5 stitches.

Sew shut, leaving a long tail of yarn. Pull the yarn tail taut to complete each remaining St by weaving it through the front loop with your yarn needle. Incorporate the yarn's end.

Embroider the cactus onto the pot.

Cactus arm: Ch 8

Row 1: Begin in the second chain from your crochet hook, and make a single crochet in the next 7 stitches. Then, chain 1 and turn your work. You should now have a row of 7 single crochets.

Rows 2 to 6: Continue by making back loop only (BLO) single crochets in the next 7 stitches. Chain 1, turn your work, and repeat this for a total of 5 rows. This will create a pattern of raised stitches on one side of your work.

Crochet row 6 and the other side of the chain.

Leave a long tail for stitching and fasten off.

Using your yarn needle, close the top of the cactus arm now, weaving the yarn tail through the top loops of each subsequent row. Sew via loops 1, 3, 5, and so on. These are the rows that the cactus has in between the rows that give it its bumps. To shut, pull it tightly. Make a little knot to secure the yarn on the opposite side of the cactus arm after pulling the yarn through the cactus to the other opening with many stitches. Stuff the cactus arm and secure it with a sewing stitch.

Flower:

Round 1: Begin with a slip stitch (slst) in the magic ring. Followed by a double crochet (dc) in the same magic ring. Repeat this pattern: slst, dc, slst, dc, slst, dc, slst, dc, slst, dc, all into the same magic ring.

Sew in the yarn end, knot the back of the flower, and fasten off with an EV.

Use green yarn to tie a french knot to create the green center section of the flower. Sew the flower onto the cactus using the green yarn.

Use the yarn to create a loop on the side of the cactus and tie a knot to conceal it behind the bloom if you want to convert it into a keychain. Your cactus keychain is now complete!

LION AMIGURUMI

Yarn:

- Beige color
- 2x Yellow color
- Brown color:
- Black color
- Synthetic Poly filling
- 1 pair safety eyes size: 10mm
- Scissors
- Tapestry needles
- Pins
- hook size 2.5 mm 4/0

Head (in yellow yarn)

Round 1: Start with a magic ring and create 6 single crochet (sc) stitches in that ring. You should have 6 stitches in this round.

Round 2: Increase (inc) in each of the 6 stitches from the previous round, resulting in 12 stitches at the end of this round.

Round 3: In each of the 12 stitches from the previous round, alternate between doing a single crochet (sc) and increasing (inc). You'll have 18 stitches after completing this round.

Round 4: In each of the 18 stitches from the previous round, follow this pattern: single crochet (sc) in the next 2 stitches, then increase (inc) in the following stitch. Repeat this sequence 6 times, and you'll end up with 24 stitches.

Round 5: Similar to the previous round, but now you'll single crochet (sc) in the next 3 stitches before increasing (inc) in the following stitch. Repeat this sequence 6 times for a total of 30 stitches.

Round 6: Continuing the pattern, single crochet (sc) in the next 4 stitches, followed by an increase (inc) in the following stitch. Repeat this sequence 6 times, resulting in 36 stitches.

Round 7: Repeat the same pattern, but this time single crochet (sc) in the next 5 stitches, followed by an increase (inc) in the following stitch. Do this 6 times to end up with 42 stitches.

Round 8: Repeat the pattern once more, single crocheting (sc) in the next 6 stitches, and increasing (inc) in the following stitch. This will give you a total of 48 stitches.

Rounds 9-10: Simply single crochet (sc) in all 48 stitches for both rounds.

Round 11: In this round, single crochet (sc) in the next 7 stitches, and then increase (inc) in the following stitch. Repeat this pattern 6 times to have a total of 54 stitches in this round.

Rounds 12-13: Single crochet (sc) in all 54 stitches for both rounds 12 and 13.

Round 14: For this round, single crochet (sc) in the next 8 stitches and then increase (inc) in the following stitch. Repeat this sequence 6 times, resulting in 60 stitches in this round.

Rounds 15-21: Single crochet (sc) in all 60 stitches for each of the following rounds from round 15 to round 21.

Insert both safety eyes between rounds 16 and 17, with an interspace of 13 stitches.

Round 22: In this round, single crochet (sc) in the next 8 stitches, and then decrease (dec) by stitching 2 stitches together. Repeat this pattern 6 times, resulting in 54 stitches in this round.

Round 23: Single crochet (sc) in the next 7 stitches, and then decrease (dec). Repeat this sequence 6 times, resulting in 48 stitches in this round.

Round 24: For this round, single crochet (sc) in the next 6 stitches, and then decrease (dec). Repeat this sequence 6 times, resulting in 42 stitches in this round.

Round 25: Single crochet (sc) in the next 5 stitches, and then decrease (dec). Repeat this sequence 6 times, resulting in 36 stitches in this round.

Round 26: For this round, single crochet (sc) in the next 4 stitches, and then decrease (dec). Repeat this sequence 6 times, resulting in 30 stitches in this round.

Round 27: Single crochet (sc) in the next 3 stitches, and then decrease (dec). Repeat this sequence 6 times, resulting in 24 stitches in this round.

Round 28: In the final round, single crochet (sc) in the next 2 stitches, and then decrease (dec). Repeat this sequence 6 times, resulting in 18 stitches in this round.

Fill the head with filling.

Round 29: In this round, single crochet (sc) in the next stitch, then decrease (dec). Repeat this pattern 6 times, resulting in 12 stitches in this round.

Round 30: The final round is all about decreasing. Decrease (dec) in each of the 6 stitches, which will leave you with just 6 stitches in this round. Once you're done with this round, you can fasten off your work.

Using the last strand of yarn, complete the head by sewing it through the front loops of each crochet St created in the previous round. To seal the hole, pull the yarn tightly. Now thread the yarn end through the hole using a needle.

Ear (in yellow yarn):

Round 1: Begin with a magic ring and crochet 6 single crochets (sc) into it. You'll have 6 stitches in this round.

Round 2: Continue with single crochets, working 1 sc into each of the 12 stitches. You'll now have 12 stitches.

Round 3: Crochet 1 sc followed by an increase (inc) into each of the 6 stitches. This will give you a total of 18 stitches in this round.

Round 4: Work a single crochet (sc) into each of the 18 stitches in this round.

Round 5: This round involves a single crochet (sc) followed by a decrease (dec) in each of the 6 stitches. This will result in a total of 12 stitches.

Round 6: Finish up with a single crochet (sc) in each of the 12 stitches in this round. Once you're done with this round, your piece is complete!

Fasten off, leaving a long tail for sewing.

Body (in yellow yarn):

Round 1: Start with a magic ring and crochet 6 single crochets (sc) into it. You will have 6 stitches.

Round 2: Increase (inc) in each of the 6 stitches. This will bring your total stitch count to 12.

Round 3: In this round, alternate between a single crochet (sc) and an increase (inc) in each of the 6 stitches. You'll now have 18 stitches.

Round 4: Crochet 2 single crochets (sc) followed by an increase (inc) in each of the 6 stitches. You'll have a total of 24 stitches.

Round 5: Continue with the pattern, working 3 single crochets (sc) followed by an increase (inc) in each of the 6 stitches. This will give you a total of 30 stitches.

Round 6: Extend the pattern by crocheting 4 single crochets (sc) followed by an increase (inc) in each of the 6 stitches, resulting in 36 stitches.

Rounds 7 to 8: Keep the pattern going by increasing and adding 6 more stitches in each round. In Round 7, do 5 single crochets (sc) followed by an increase (inc) in each of the 6 stitches. In Round 8, work 6 single crochets (sc) followed by an increase (inc) in each of the 6 stitches. Your stitch count will be 42 in Round 7 and 48 in Round 8.

Rounds 9 to 19: For the next 10 rounds, maintain a total of 54 stitches in each round by single crocheting (sc) in all 54 stitches.

Round 20: In this round, you'll single crochet (sc) in the next 7 stitches, then make a decrease (dec). Repeat this pattern 6 times, and you'll have 48 stitches at the end of this round.

Rounds 21 to 23: Continue to single crochet (sc) in all 48 stitches for the next 3 rounds.

Round 24: Now, crochet 6 single crochets (sc) followed by a decrease (dec) in each of the 6 stitches. Your stitch count will reduce to 42.

Rounds 25 to 27: For the next 3 rounds, maintain a stitch count of 42 by single crocheting (sc) in all 42 stitches.

Round 28: In this round, work 5 single crochets (sc) followed by a decrease (dec) in each of the 6 stitches, bringing your stitch count to 36.

Round 29: In the final round, single crochet (sc) in all 36 stitches.

Leave a long tail for stitching and fasten off. Pack the body full of fiberfill. St the head and body together in the intervals of 9 and 26 rounds.

We will now create a single layer of hair surrounding the head.

Sections of brown yarn, 4 in./10 cm. Secure the loops by pulling two yarn strands through each other and tying a knot.

Every hair must be positioned exactly adjacent to every other hair while creating the lion's first layer of hair. You are allowed to skip a St in between each hair in the following hair round. Once you have all the hairs, you won't notice this.

Sewing is required for the ears behind the first row of hair, in between the second row's hairs. Between rounds 6 and 12 of the head, the ears are sewn on.

You may now begin creating the last portion of the mane by skipping a few stitches. Hair should cover the head completely to the neck.

Snout (make 2, in beige yarn)

Round 1: Begin by making 6 single crochet (sc) stitches into a magic ring. This is your starting point with 6 stitches.

Round 2: In the second round, increase (inc) in each of the 6 stitches. This will give you a total of 12 stitches in this round.

Rounds 3-4: For the next two rounds, simply single crochet (sc) in all 12 stitches. Maintain the stitch count at 12 stitches for these rounds

Round 5: In this round, single crochet (sc) in the next 3 stitches, then decrease (dec) 3 times. Finally, single crochet (sc) in the last 3 stitches. This will result in 9 stitches in this round.

Leave a long tail for stitching and fasten off.

St together the fifth round after filling the snout halves somewhat.

On the fifth round of the snout, embroider the nose using black yarn.

110

St the muzzle below the round 15 mark, midway between the eyes on the head.

Front Leg (make 2, in yellow yarn):

Round 1: To begin, make 6 single crochet (sc) stitches in a magic ring. You should now have 6 stitches in your first round.

Round 2: In the second round, increase (inc) in each of the 6 stitches. This will result in a total of 12 stitches in this round.

Round 3: In the third round, alternate between making a single crochet (sc) and increasing (inc) in the next stitch. Repeat this pattern 6 times, giving you a total of 18 stitches in this round.

Round 4: In round 4, single crochet (sc) in the next 2 stitches, and then increase (inc) in the following stitch. Repeat this sequence 6 times, so you'll have 24 stitches in this round.

Rounds 5-8: Continue to single crochet (sc) in each of the 24 stitches for the next 4 rounds. Maintain a stitch count of 24 in each of these rounds.

Round 9: In round 9, single crochet (sc) in the next 2 stitches, and then decrease (dec) in the following stitch. Repeat this pattern 6 times, resulting in 18 stitches in this round.

Rounds 10-11: Continue by single crocheting (sc) in all 18 stitches for the next 2 rounds, maintaining a stitch count of 18 in each round.

Round 12: In the 12th round, single crochet (sc) in the next 4 stitches, and then decrease (dec) in the following stitch. Repeat this sequence 3 times, resulting in a total of 15 stitches in this round.

Rounds 13-21: For the next 9 rounds (rounds 13 to 21), simply make a single crochet (sc) in all 15 stitches in each of these rounds, maintaining a consistent stitch count of 15 throughout.

Fill the legs with fiberfilling.

Round 22: In the 22nd round, single crochet (sc) in the next 3 stitches, then decrease (dec) in the following stitch. Repeat this sequence 3 times, and you'll have a total of 12 stitches in this round.

Round 23: In the final 23rd round, decrease (dec) in each of the 6 stitches, reducing your stitch count to 6 stitches in total. This should complete your project.

Using the final strand of yarn, complete the front leg by sewing it through the front loops of each crochet St created in the previous round. To seal the hole, pull the yarn tightly. Now thread the yarn end through the hole using a needle.

Hindleg (make 2, in yellow yarn)

Round 1: You start by creating a circle with 6 single crochet (sc) stitches. This forms the center of your work.

Round 2: In this round, you're going to increase the number of stitches. Do this by making 2 sc in each of the 6 stitches from the previous round, giving you a total of 12 stitches.

Round 3: For this round, you'll alternate between 1 sc and an increase (inc) in the next stitch. You do this 6 times, resulting in a total of 18 stitches.

Round 4: Now, you'll single crochet in the next 2 stitches and then increase in the following stitch. Repeat this 6 times, giving you a total of 24 stitches.

Rounds 5-8: These rounds are simple. You just make 1 single crochet in each of the 24 stitches from the previous round.

Round 9: Similar to Rnd 3, you'll alternate stitches, but this time you're doing 2 single crochets and then a decrease (dec) in the next stitch. Repeat this 6 times, reducing the stitch count to 18.

Rounds 10-11: In these rounds, you continue to make 1 single crochet in each of the 18 stitches.

Round 12: In this round, you'll single crochet in the next 4 stitches, and then make a decrease (dec) in the next stitch. Repeat this pattern 3 times, and you'll end up with 15 stitches.

Rounds 13-16: For these rounds, simply single crochet in each of the 15 stitches. This maintains the stitch count.

Round 17: Now, alternate between single crocheting in the next 4 stitches and making an increase (inc) in the following stitch. Repeat this pattern 3 times, giving you a total of 18 stitches.

Round 18: Similar to the previous round, you'll single crochet in the next 5 stitches and then increase in the next stitch. Do this 3 times, and you'll have 21 stitches.

Rounds 19-21: These rounds are straightforward. Just single crochet in all 21 stitches for each round.

Round 22: In this round, alternate between single crocheting in the next 5 stitches and making a decrease (dec) in the next stitch. Repeat this pattern 3 times, and you'll be left with 18 stitches.

Stuff the legs with fiberfilling.

Round 23: For this round, you'll alternate between making a single crochet (sc) in the next stitch and making a decrease (dec) in the following stitch. Repeat this pattern 6 times, and you'll have 12 stitches left at the end of this round.

Round 24: In this final round, you'll make a decrease (dec) in each of the 6 stitches. This will bring your stitch count down to 6.

Using the remaining strand of yarn, finish the hindleg by sewing it through the front loops of each crochet St created in the previous round. To seal the hole, pull the yarn tightly. Now thread the yarn end through the hole using a needle.

Toes for leg 12x (in yellow yarn):

Round 1: Begin by creating 6 single crochet (sc) stitches in a magic ring. This forms the center of your work with 6 stitches.

Round 2: In this round, alternate between making a single crochet (sc) in the next stitch and increasing (inc) in the following stitch. Repeat this pattern 3 times, and you'll have a total of 9 stitches in this round.

Round 3: Crochet a single crochet (sc) in each of the 9 stitches in this round.

Leave a long tail for stitching and fasten off.

In between rounds 4 and 9, sew three toes adjacent to each other on one leg. For the last 3 legs, repeat.

Small paw pad for leg 12x (in beige yarn):

Round 1: To begin, create 4 single crochet (sc) stitches in a magic ring. This will give you a circle with 4 stitches.

Leave a long tail for stitching and fasten off. The little paw pads should be sewn under the toes

Big paw pad for leg 4x (in beige yarn):

Round 1: Begin by making 8 single crochet (sc) stitches in a magic ring. This will form a circle with 8 stitches.

Leave a long tail for stitching and fasten off. Sew the huge paw pads onto each leg's first round.

Sew the front legs between rounds 24 and 29 on the side of the body.

In the space between rounds 9 and 14, sew the hindlegs to the side of the torso.

Tail (in yellow yarn):

Round 1: Start by making 6 single crochet (sc) stitches in a magic ring. This will create a small circle with 6 stitches.

Rounds 2 to 9: Continue to single crochet in each of the 6 stitches in every round for a total of 8 rounds.

Leave a long tail for stitching and fasten off.

Just like you did for the head, add some hair to the tail's rounds 1, 3, and 4. I trimmed the hairs a little shorter than the head hair. Sew the tail to the body at the intervals of rounds 8–11.

Your lion is finished now.

CONCLUSION

You may be wondering if crocheting is for you before deciding if you want to invest the time to learn. Depending on your personality and the available resources, learning to crochet can be simple. Some pick up crocheting quickly and can create a huge blanket on their first attempt. Some might require a bit more experience. Your mindset about it is what matters. You have to work at learning crochet if you want it to be simple. If you want to improve, practicing is essential.

The amount of time you have to practice will determine how long it takes you to learn how to crochet. In the coming days, you may pick up the fundamentals of crocheting if you have at least an hour of free time every day.

If you've already begun dabbling with crochet, you might be wondering what a novice like you should crochet. Working on crochet projects that simply require the fundamental stitches is the greatest method to practice.

It's a fantastic method to enhance mental wellness in addition to being beneficial for your real brain. You might not be aware of this if you haven't spent much time here. I was under a lot of stress at the time, which is the main reason I chose to learn how to crochet.

My life altered drastically the minute I produced my first pair of fingerless gloves. I enjoyed creating, giving, and learning new things, and I was happier and more upbeat.

Ever since, it has consistently helped me feel less anxious on my bad days, and I've heard so many positive stories from so many different individuals. You should definitely try this if you suffer from sadness or anxiety.

Typically, learning to crochet isn't done with the intention of being financially successful. But that is very much conceivable! I work full-time from home as a crocheter, and I couldn't be happier.

There are several ways to make it into a side business when you're ready:

- blogging
- selling your designs
- submitting your designs to magazines
- working with yarn companies
- selling physical items online or at craft fairs
- hand-dying and selling yarn

Good luck friend.

BONUS

BONUS 1

BONUS 2

BONUS 3

Made in the USA
Las Vegas, NV
05 April 2024

88289685R00063